BE A WINNER

Richard Orr is the editor and co-creator of www.inthewinningzone. com. He has an MSc with Distinction in Journalism from Napier University and is a former winner of the BBC Young Sports Reporter of the Year award. Richard is a keen and competitive sportsman, playing football, rugby and squash.

Kenny Kemp is an award-winning newspaper journalist with over 25 years' experience. He was Business Journalist of the Year in Scotland in 2001 and 2003. He has worked on *The Scotsman*, *Scotland on Sunday*, the *London Evening Standard* and the *Sunday Herald*. He is also an author and won the WHSmith Business Book Award in 2004 as co-author of *Go: An Airline Adventure*, with Barbara Cassani.

The publication of *Be a Winner* has been generously supported by Cairn Energy plc (www.cairn-energy.plc.uk). Cairn is one of Europe's largest independent oil and gas exploration and production companies listed on the London Stock Exchange and is based in Edinburgh, Scotland.

BE A WINNER

Achieve Your Goals with Scotland's Sporting Heroes

Richard Orr and Kenny Kemp
Foreword by Sir Alex Ferguson

In partnership with
WINNING SCOTLAND FOUNDATION

MAINSTREAM
PUBLISHING

EDINBURGH AND LONDON

First published in Great Britain in 2008 by
MAINSTREAM PUBLISHING COMPANY
(EDINBURGH) LTD
7 Albany Street
Edinburgh EH1 3UG

ISBN 9781845964023

A catalogue record for this book is available
from the British Library

Typeset in Caslon and Gill Sans

Printed in Great Britain by
Clays Ltd, St Ives plc

CONTENTS

BE A WINNER – THAT IS ALMOST A metaphor for my life. By that, I mean I have always tried to perform to my best ability anything I've taken up or attempted to perform, whether in sport or life in general. One has to have a drive within oneself, as no one will do it for you.

Of course, you will always have a great teacher, an inspirational coach, or a father, mother, sister or brother to look up to and point you in the right direction. But, if that crumb of ambition is not there within you, you cannot learn that. I have always said that about the best players that have played under me at teams such as Aberdeen and then Manchester United.

Willie Miller and Roy Keane – my respective captains at those clubs – were players I genuinely trusted 100 per cent on the football field, as they had that desire to succeed and drive themselves and their team-mates on to greater endeavours. That's what made them winners in my book. With sport today, youngsters have a great deal of activities to choose from, no doubt about that. But equally the variety of other social activities available nowadays has eaten into the time you have to enjoy and later exploit the talent you may well have for any one particular sport. I was keen for my own sons to take up a sport, as long as they enjoyed it, and of course I hope the same for my grandchildren.

Bottom line, sport can teach you how to conduct yourself in life, maintain a healthy lifestyle and of course provide lifelong friends. I feel the work that the Winning Scotland Foundation conducts today is invaluable, as we need all youngsters to learn the importance of wanting to do the best they possibly can in life.

What I hope this book will provide is a guide to show you that with hard work you can achieve great things in life. I hope that you will be inspired to really challenge yourself by the interviews with some of our biggest sporting heroes today. They all say the same thing: I enjoy what I do, so I do it and nothing gets in my way. That is a strong message and one I personally endorse.

Sir Alex Ferguson

THANK YOU FOR PICKING UP *BE A WINNER*; we hope that you enjoy it. This book was inspired by our work with In The Winning Zone, a website that celebrates the achievements of Scottish athletes and coaches.

In The Winning Zone is part of the Winning Scotland Foundation, a charitable organisation that aims to create a positive winning attitude in Scotland, with sport as the catalyst. Our vision is to increase understanding and appreciation of Scotland's sporting heroes, and that as a result, more of us will aspire to win and succeed in our own lives.

None of the individuals and teams you read about in these pages made it to the top of their game without a fight. It took hard work, determination, sacrifice and fierce motivation. That's where winning comes from. And that's the message we want to put out there: that to be like these stars, you don't have to be superhuman, you just need the will and the desire. And that doesn't just apply to sport, it is relevant to career, education, business, family, health, anything.

Please visit www.inthewinningzone.com to access more exclusive interviews with Scotland's winners, our uniquely Scottish, up-to-the-minute sports news service, and our interactive sports community, Sportspace, where you can add your thoughts to the winning debate.

By doing so, you will be helping us reach our goal of making Scotland a nation of healthy, happy, positive thinkers – a nation of winners.

Richard Orr and Kenny Kemp

WHY YOU SHOULD READ THIS BOOK

DON'T YOU THINK YOU SHOULD BE FAIR TO YOURSELF? That means working out what you'd really like to do with your life. Do people put you down and tell you to 'Shut up', or say, 'Don't kid yourself, pal?' Do you expect other people to tell you what to do? Are you constantly waiting for someone else to get things started before you follow? This book is about encouraging you to stop for a moment and think about what YOU want to do with your life. The opportunities are endless for those who truly want to open their eyes and make a go of life.

There's something desperately negative about the way many Scots look at life. That really has to change. And you have it in your power to change. Ask yourself the question: *Would I like the opportunity to do something special and worthwhile with my life?*

That's what *Be a Winner* is all about. We've used the actual words of Scotland's great sporting achievers to prove something to you: that talent takes you only so far in life. After that, you need to add application and hard work. And the rub of good luck. All the sportspeople in *Be a Winner* have used their own natural talent and ability, but have been prepared to work to achieve their goals. To make something better and much more fulfilling of our lives is a choice available to every one of us, whatever our background, whatever the barriers placed in our way.

While this book is aimed at young people, please don't put it down if you're in your twenties, or if you're a parent, grandparent or teacher. You are never too old to set some goals in life and try to achieve them. Your life is already too precious and short. Even if you're a 90 year old, you can set a little target for something to be achieved this week. Then you can go for it. It is meant to be enjoyable, too!

Be a Winner is about being much more positive and determined. We don't think there has ever been a book like this in Scotland. We've spoken to well over 100 committed athletes and coaches – including some very famous people indeed – and asked them for their thoughts and beliefs on winning. While they all share certain traits, such as unwavering doggedness, each is an individual with a desire to do well and his or her own special way of rising to the challenges they have faced.

By reading this book, we want you to *Be a Winner*, too. This might not mean winning a gold medal for Scotland in the Commonwealth Games in Glasgow in 2014 (although that would be fantastic), but what it does mean is achieving something worthwhile, reaching for your personal best. This book is about *you* setting goals for yourself in sport and life – and then achieving these goals.

Of course, the opposite of this is being a loser. That's the kind of street insult you hear regularly in Scotland: 'You're a loser.' But it is possible to turn this around – it starts with nothing more than a few tiny steps forward, and often it takes time to stick with it. In this book, you will hear from a range of Scotland's finest sportspeople. Often, they have faced setbacks and disappointments, but this is all part and parcel of the journey to *Be a Winner*.

Why have we written this book? *Be a Winner* is the brainchild of the Winning Scotland Foundation, a charity set up by Sir Bill Gammell, the former Scottish international rugby player and now a successful international business leader with Cairn Energy plc. From the Foundation has come the outstanding Scottish sports website, www. inthewinningzone.com, now supporting and highlighting all kinds of sporting excellence across Scotland. But the Foundation's role in creating a culture of winning is much wider and deeper – it is to encourage *everyone* to think and act like a winner in life.

We all have our dreams. And no one has the right to destroy your dreams. So, if you want to play rugby, football, squash, tennis, hockey or golf for Scotland, then work towards that dream every day. It might well become a reality. If the sporting people in the following pages are able to inspire you, then *Be a Winner* has done its job.

I

I AM – INSPIRATION, AMBITION, MOTIVATION

'He is the ultimate athlete, the personification of class and dedication. And all that hard work has paid off.'

The tearful BBC commentator Hugh Porter, after track cyclist Chris Hoy became the first Briton in 54 years to win the men's sprint world title, Manchester, 28 March 2008

THERE ARE FEW ATHLETES IN THE WORLD WHO can emulate what Chris Hoy has achieved. In becoming a double world-record holder, Olympic gold medallist and a grand-slam world champion (the kilo, keirin and sprint), Hoy has succeeded in attaining the holy trinity of sporting feats. He is the very best in the world at what he does. He is also Scottish.

But what made him this way? Was he born to win? Was he driven ever harder to succeed by people around him? Was he surrounded by all the slick facilities and expensive coaches necessary to make him a winner on the world stage?

It would be reassuring if the answer to all these questions was yes. It's natural to think that the guys who become the top dogs, the real deal, were lucky to be in the right place at the right time. But, as it happens, none of that applies to Chris Hoy.

HOW I LOVED RUNNING FROM THE VERY START, BY ANDREW LEMONCELLO

British and Scottish steeplechase champion Andrew Lemoncello explains how just the pure fun of it made him follow a career in distance running.

'I was always pretty sporty and I always loved sport,' says Andrew. 'But when I was 12 my mum took a few people along to a championship and I came seventh in my first race. In the long term, I joined the club that I am with now — Fife Athletics Club — and a couple of weeks later I was in my first cross-country race and came in joint first as a Scottish champion!

'I loved it, and it has always been a highlight of my week. Tuesdays and Thursdays were my school training days, and it was so much fun, I couldn't wait for those days.

'If I didn't enjoy it, I wouldn't do it. It's not what keeps me going, but it's what makes me tick, because I love getting up in the morning and running. If I don't do a run in the morning, it's not that I can't function, but my body just feels different from normal. I feel so much better knowing that I have been out there and done something. You will find that with a lot of runners.'

The term 'Born Winner' might have been coined by the Scottish headline writers, but Hoy has slogged his guts out, forcing his body to work so hard that, at times, he passes out from sheer exhaustion, to become the illustrious athlete he is today. Twenty years ago, there was little to suggest what was to come from Hoy. Growing up in Edinburgh, he was just a normal kid with a regular life, facing the same challenges as the rest of us.

He may be a muscle-bound six-footer now, but at school Hoy was one of the smaller kids. He found it tough, but it served him well, especially on the rugby pitch. 'I used to take a right pasting,' he recalls. 'I was playing stand-off. I was the smallest guy on the team, and I was getting the back-row forwards peeling off the scrum and running straight at me. But that worked for me, because I had to work so much harder just to stay level with these guys.'

He did a spot of rowing as well, which he was very good at, before deciding to switch to cycling full-time in his late teens. 'When I was 17, I was rowing and cycling for Scotland. There was a chance I could have gone for rowing, but I wasn't big enough, so I never would have made it as a rower at a higher level. Cycling appealed more because I had more control over what I was doing. You didn't have a four- or an eight-man team. You put the work in and you got the results.'

As you can see, the young Chris Hoy had the same hopes and aspirations as many young men and women. There was no reason to suggest he was destined to become the person he is today. At 17, he was obviously a decent athlete, but he wasn't outstanding. Chris knew this.

'I had always felt I was good enough at sport but not exceptionally good. There were always guys, whether it was cycling, rowing or rugby, who were something special, real talented kids. I thought to myself that I could be competitive and right up there, but I never thought I could be as good as these guys in terms of raw talent.

'Maybe because they were so gifted and won so easily, they didn't really have the desire to work hard when they had to, and they also didn't like the feeling of losing when it happened. So, perhaps being the nearly man, getting seconds and thirds, doing all the right things but not necessarily being the best, gave me the desire to keep going and see how far I could go. Who knows? Maybe if I was winning by a mile as a kid I wouldn't still be doing it now,' he says.

So even Chris Hoy, when talking about growing up, admits he wasn't an extraordinary individual. He didn't see any signs in himself that suggested he would go on to be one of the best, barely a decade later. But what he had was the right attitude. He wasn't a quitter, and he would stand his ground and try his best. So, for all that he may have lacked in natural talent and even in physicality as a youngster, Hoy made up for it in other ways. He had the essence of a true winner. He had the 'I AM' mindset.

What is 'I AM'? Well, it is both philosophical and literal. I AM is who you are and what fuels your desires. Within your inner depths, it defines who you are and what you might become. I AM, literally, is your *Inspiration, Ambition and Motivation*. Hoy's I AM was to be the best he could be. Nothing lofty but nothing unattainable, either.

'I had always dreamed of being an Olympic champion, but I never thought I was going to be one,' he says. 'As a kid, I never put myself in the same bracket as the guys who were winning medals at the top level, but what I did do was set myself targets.'

Just because he didn't think he could win the Olympics didn't mean he wouldn't try to be the best he could be. He decided to see how far he could go, one step at a time. That was his inspiration, his ambition and his motivation all rolled into one.

'I said I wanted to be Scottish champion, so I did it. Then I said I wanted to be British champion, so I did that, too. It's always come from setting myself a target. "Is it do-able?" I ask. "I don't know, but I'm going to give it my best possible shot." Then, even if I don't make it, I know how far I can go. If you keep resetting your goals and you keep hitting them, eventually you will reach the top.'

THE GOLDEN MOMENT THAT DEFINED SCOTTISH RUNNER ROSEMARY STIRLING

Rosemary Wright paid an emotional visit back to Scotland, the land of her heritage and greatest triumph, in 2008. The native New Zealander — who ran for Scotland — was there as coach to the Kiwi cross-country team, in Edinburgh for the World Championships.

As she peered out over Meadowbank Stadium, she recalled the glorious day in July 1970 when she — as Rosemary Stirling — and her then boyfriend, Ian Stewart, won Commonwealth golds for Scotland on the athletics track. Rosemary stormed past England's Pat Low and Cheryl Peasley of Australia in the 800m, while Stewart beat fellow Scot Ian McCafferty in the 5,000m.

'I wasn't favourite to win,' she told *The Scotsman*. 'The favourite was Sheila Carey, but she tripped and fell. I wasn't really aware of that because I was in front of her, and it wasn't until the finishing line that I found out who had fallen. My most vivid memory is from about 150 metres from the finish, and the piercing screaming and yelling of the crowd ringing in my ears. Pat Low and Cheryl Peasley and myself were going for the finish line, the three of us in a row. When I won, it was quite surreal.'

It was a magical day for her — and for the Scots who recall her triumph. But it could have been very different if it weren't for her relationship with Ian. He gave her an 'I AM' moment that turned to gold at Meadowbank. 'I'd attribute a lot of it to Ian, because he was quite different from me. He was so single-minded. He lived for running, and I became a bit like that,' she said. I AM comes from many different places . . .

Hoy also insists that he was driven by his parents. But when he says 'driven', he doesn't mean that they pushed him into sport and pressured him into competing and succeeding. He means he was supported by them, and most of the 'driving' was in his dad's car.

'The motivation came from me, but my parents were always there to support me, which was fantastic. I'm always keen to emphasise that for me it was never the pushy-parent approach. I was in BMX from the age of seven, and it was really competitive. I saw kids at BMX that came off the track in tears and their mums and dads were shouting at them and giving them a smack about the head! They were hating it, and I was the opposite. I was begging my parents to take me to this place and that place. I spent my whole time thinking about racing my bike, and they were just there to support me and give me the best opportunities.

'If they hadn't been as supportive, there is no way I would be where I am now, purely because it takes a massive investment of time and money to get a kid going in these types of sports. BMX had races in Southampton one weekend and then Inverness the next. One year, my dad did 30,000 miles driving me around Britain to different races!'

Hoy's reason for racing when he was a kid was that he enjoyed it. That's how his I AM moment developed and grew, and it is what keeps him going every day. 'If I didn't enjoy it, there would be nothing to keep me motivated,' he claims.

The effort required to excel in track cycling is gargantuan. It is days, weeks and months of soul-sucking, sinew-straining training for what usually amounts to less than a minute of action in a competitive race.

PUTTING I AM INTO ACTION

Hoy is a proven champion, but what he says – 'If I didn't enjoy it, there would be nothing to keep me motivated' – could be a quote from anyone, talking about anything. It could be from a teacher who arrives at work each morning confronted by dozens of yelling, brawling, hyperactive kids. Or it could be from a shivering fisherman who sets out into a blustery sea on a treacherous winter morning. At its core, motivation is a fairly simple notion: to have the I AM factor is to want to do something, and to enjoy doing it.

However, there is a difference between being inspired, ambitious and motivated, and then actually going out and doing something about it. Because I AM is only the first step. Chris Hoy loves cycling and wants to do it – that's his I AM in a nutshell. But motivation for Hoy went beyond simply wanting to cycle. He wanted to be the best sprint cyclist in the world. He set himself targets and reached them. It didn't come easy. He had to endure many obstacles on the path to achieving his dreams. Hoy's accolades are the product of years and years of preparation, with bumps along the way, which, on a narrow-wheeled track bike with no brakes, make for some pretty uncomfortable riding.

To begin with, Hoy has been forced to suffer far from favourable conditions in order to reach the zenith of the cycling world. In his early twenties, his enthusiasm to succeed might have ebbed away because of the lack of support he and his team-mates received, the non-existence of training facilities and the absence of consistency in their competitive preparations.

'In the beginning, there were no sprint coaches in Britain at the time, and we were really just doing it on guesswork,' he explained. 'Myself, Craig MacLean and the other sprinters in that group were self-coached. We coached ourselves and coached each other. We were competing at British national level, and there was no one to guide us, no advice. We had nothing. In terms of facilities, you would spend the summer months on the track and then come September and October you would stop, and by March or April you would be back to square one. You would progress only to fall back again.'

BATTLING THROUGH THE HARD TIMES

Instead of letting it get him down, Hoy set himself a target to get through the tough times. 'Because the standard [of the British set-up] wasn't that high, I thought I maybe could make the Olympics. It was the big carrot for me.'

And his years of carrot-chasing paid off. He made the Olympics. But his gold medal came at the second time of asking. Hoy won silver at the Sydney Olympics in 2000 in the team sprint. No mean feat, but for Hoy it wasn't about winning silver but losing the gold.

'If you are winning, it is all right,' explains Hoy, 'because you can justify all the hours and hours of work and sacrifice that go along with that. But it is a tough event if you don't win it. You can put in four years of work and only get a silver or bronze at the Olympics. That might still be a massive achievement, but if what you are looking for is a gold medal and you have put four years' work in and you don't get it, it is hard to deal with.'

However, it is an essential component in an athlete's mindset to deal with adversity, as Hoy did. He believes that just because it didn't happen this time, it doesn't mean that it can't be done. Coping with disappointment, and consolidating it to come back even stronger the next time, has been vital in Hoy's career. He could have given up after coming so close first time round, but he didn't; he kept on going. Without that singular, clear target of a gold medal and nothing less, he might never have made it.

Therefore, the key to successful I AM is not just to want to do something but to set yourself a target that details how well you want to do it, and then prepare and execute an action plan to ensure that target is reached, no matter what. 'You stick at it and plug away,' says Hoy.

Chris Hoy's story is an inspiring and fitting example of what correct motivation, channelled in an appropriate and carefully planned way, can achieve. There will be bumps on the road, but by keeping your eye on the ultimate goal, your own I AM will carry you over them.

As we have found, Chris Hoy is just a normal Scottish guy with big dreams. It may be unrealistic to think we can all aspire to achieve on the same level as he has, but the beauty of I AM is that your target does not need to be grand or lofty, and whether it is to do the Caledonian Challenge, the MoonWalk or the Pedal for Scotland bike ride between Edinburgh and Glasgow, we all have some level of I AM within us.

WHERE DOES I AM COME FROM?

I AM is different things to different people. Chris Hoy was motivated by a love of cycling, but the willingness of his parents to nurture his passion gave him a push in the right direction.

Every Scottish winner has his or her own story to tell.

Snooker stars Stephen Hendry and Stephen Maguire each received a little bit of I AM from a variety of sources. Hendry acknowledges several I AM factors that built him up to become a seven-times world champion and the most successful snooker player ever to have lived.

'I just knew I was good, but it wasn't until I met Ian Doyle [his manager] that I realised how good I might be . . . because he kept telling me,' explains Hendry. 'I think there are lots of things to consider: if I hadn't got a table from Santa, would I have taken up snooker? Would I have been as disciplined if I hadn't met Ian? Would I have been the youngest-ever world champion if I hadn't experienced the Crucible a few times before I reached a final? I think there are lots of things that shape a career.'

Maguire, a European Open winner and UK Championship finalist, has a more specific story to tell. When he was young, he was so keen to play that his grandparents didn't just buy him a snooker table, they actually knocked a wall out of their home to make room for it so he could play.

'It was a huge sacrifice on their part, and one I could never thank them enough for,' Maguire says. 'I remember thinking it was a great idea, but then the local paper got hold of the story and that's when I kind of realised that this wasn't normal . . . it was something special they had done.'

Kirsty Balfour, on the other hand, puts her I AM factor down to God. A devout Christian, the Commonwealth and European champion swimmer dedicates every race to pleasing her creator. In fact, if it wasn't for her faith, she doesn't think she could cope with the demands of her sport.

'I do feel it as a kind of duty. I believe that God is helping me to do it, so if I get lazy and don't try, then I feel it is disrespectful to what He wants me to be doing. He has given me the strength to come this far, and He has plans for my future. So I have to keep working hard at it. Even the ability to train is a gift, and the motivation, determination and sacrifice is not something that comes easily. The things I have to push my body to do every day are beyond what I think I may be otherwise capable of.'

HOW ABOUT THIS FOR INSPIRATION? OVER 40 YEARS ON – WHY THE LISBON LIONS REMAIN SCOTLAND'S GREATEST TEAM

The debate in Scotland will rage for generations — and there are many suitable contenders. But what was the greatest Scottish sporting team? There can be few who will not agree that Jock Stein's Celtic — the Lisbon Lions of 1967 — must be at the top of the list. Celtic were the first British football team to win the European Cup — now the Champions League — in 1967, a year before the all-stars of Manchester United (with Scots Denis Law and manager Matt Busby playing key roles) took the trophy at Wembley, against Benfica.

When Jock Stein, the manager of Dunfermline Athletic, returned to Celtic Park in 1965 as the boss, the Glasgow team was in disarray. But Stein managed to mould a group of players into a team of superstars with the ability and self-confidence to take on — and beat — the best in the world. The 2–1 victory over Inter Milan in Lisbon remains a benchmark for a Scottish team. Every one of the team was born in Scotland and all within a few miles of Parkhead.

What made them successful was a blend of mental toughness and resolve in defence, creative movement and pinpoint passing in the middle, and the clinical finishing to see off even the toughest opponents. The Lisbon Lions also had room for the wayward genius of Jimmy Johnstone — who fitted in because the rest of the team gave him the space to perform. The Lisbon Lions had it all — and remain to this day an example of Scots who wanted to be winners.

Similarly, celebrated Scottish sprinter Eric Liddell had unflinching faith in the gift given to him by God. So much so that when he heard that the 100m heats for the 1924 Olympics were to be held on a Sunday, he pulled out of the event, upholding the Christian ethic that the Sabbath was to be a day of rest. Instead, he took up the 400m, an event that wasn't alien to him, but not one was he an expert at. It was a decision met with scepticism by his peers and rivals. To draw a modern comparison, no one would expect Donovan Bailey to have defeated Michael Johnson over 400m in the 1996 Olympics, nor Tyson Gay to upset Jeremy Wariner if they were to race over 400m in 2008.

Just before the 400m final was about to start, and after Liddell had shaken every one of his opponents' hands, an American masseur slipped a piece of paper into his hand. On it was written a verse from 1 Samuel: 'Those who honour me, I will honour.' So at least one other person on earth had faith in him.

In the end, Liddell won the race emphatically and in doing so broke the world record, with a time of 47.6 seconds to take the gold medal for Great Britain. It remains one of the most outstanding and moving moments in the history of sport.

In February 2008, Scottish minister John Keddie published the book *Running the Race*, which depicts Liddell's efforts as he prepares to take on the best in the world in an event that he was unaccustomed to, certainly compared with his opponents. In it, Keddie says:

> This was an event he had very little experience in. But in Paris he devastated the field, dominated the race. It was magnified by the fact he was in the outside lane. It was a *Boy's Own* tale that was real.

Liddell's story is legendary. Some draw inspiration from his commitment to his faith, others from the pure effort and determination he summoned to 'devastate' a field of runners vastly more experienced in that specific event than he was.

Andy Murray, Scotland's star tennis player – who thrilled the public with his staggering comeback against Frenchman Richard Gasquet in the fourth round of Wimbledon 2008 – grew up watching one of sport's greatest rivalries unfold on the tennis courts – Pete Sampras versus Andre Agassi, who battled it out for years to be hailed the world's greatest player. Much of his inspiration came from watching Agassi in action. Murray idolised him, to the extent that he literally modelled himself on him – an I AM moment that led him to his decision that moving abroad would further his chances of succeeding.

'When I was very young, I just enjoyed playing and was inspired by Andre Agassi. I loved watching him play and I had all his gear – the denim shorts with the pink Lycra shorts underneath and I even had a Nike cap with a blond ponytail attached to it. When I was 14, I realised I wanted to become a tennis player, and I chose to leave Scotland and base myself in Spain. That's when I really started to focus on being the best I could be, and the motivation was all internal.'

Glasgow athlete Lee McConnell, who won a bronze medal with the British 4x400m relay team at the 2007 IAAF World Athletics Championships in Osaka, Japan, found her way into running simply because she loved sport. As a youngster, she got involved in everything she could and eventually found that athletics was the track she should go down.

'From a young age, I always enjoyed sport. I did swimming, netball, ice skating – a huge amount of different varieties. I did summer athletics at primary school and through to secondary school. I then went to various summer camps where you could go and try the different events. I went with a high-jump coach who then took me on as a high jumper and it all snowballed from there. I joined the City of Glasgow Athletics Club, which was great; growing up doing all the competitions – it was fantastic.

'Being naturally quite good at athletics, it started taking up more of my time, which meant I didn't have any time for the other sports. It really just evolved; I was never pushed into it, and it naturally happened. I found myself enjoying it more and more, and being quite successful at it helps you decide what you want to do.'

TURNING I AM INTO WINNING

Scottish duathlete Catriona Morrison has a simple outlook on her career. She wants to win. In December 2006, she said, 'There are two things that I want to do. I want to win the European title next year in Edinburgh, and I'd like to win the world title.'

Admittedly, not at the top of everyone's priority list, but that's what did it for her. She had set herself two very clear, obvious goals, and they would be the motivation for the torturous lifestyle to which she committed herself in a bid to achieve them.

Throughout the whole winter of 2006–07, Morrison, from Broxburn, would run 10km and cycle 40km laps round Arthur's Seat in Edinburgh, preparing for the European Championships she would compete for on home soil. She battled through freezing rain, slushy sleet and the rampaging Scottish winds – often, to avoid the heavy traffic, before

HOW BABE ZAHARIAS CAPTURED THE HEART OF SCOTLAND

One of the greatest all-round female athletes wasn't born in Scotland, but she is still remembered with affection as an inspiration in golfing circles.

Babe Didrikson Zaharias, born in Texas in 1911, won two gold medals, for javelin and the 80m sprint, and one silver medal, for the high jump, in the 1932 Los Angeles Olympics. She established world records that remained unbeaten for many years.

Then, in 1935, she took up golf, a latecomer to the sport. But her determination to succeed and her natural ability were legendary. She won 82 professional and amateur championships, including the British Women's Open golf championship at Gullane in 1947 — the first American to do so since the tournament began in 1893.

It made her a national celebrity in the UK and even today her achievement, and the excitement it caused, is still recalled in East Lothian. Her name was even given to one of Scotland's top competitions for women's golf — The Babe Zaharias Trophy in Whitekirk. In 1949, she was the first woman to be signed up for a major sports sponsorship deal. Golf legend Bobby Jones reckoned she was one of the top ten golfers — male or female — of all time.

most of Edinburgh had woken up – ensuring that she had the track mastered to perfection.

She complained, she hated it, but every day she still got up to do it. 'I just want a life; it sucks,' she moaned. 'There are some mornings that I find it almost impossible to get up. I feel I just can't do it; I don't want to do it. When you are working seven hours a day, I can see why people look forward to the weekend, but I don't particularly look forward to my weekend because I know there is a five-hour bike ride in there among other stuff.'

So why does she do it?

'I owe it to myself, it makes me feel good to do it, and I get a lot of self-satisfaction. I feel like I'm proving myself. I am also motivated by knowing that all my opponents are out there doing it, too.'

When the European Championships came round on 16 June, it just happened to be in the midst of Britain's worst summer for decades, and this particular Saturday was no exception. Winter hats and raincoats were the apparel of choice for the few hundred enthusiasts who braved the elements to watch. Meanwhile, Catriona was destroying her opposition. She was in a field of world-class athletes, but her ultimate desire to win on home soil shone through, and she could have walked the last few hundred yards of the race and still crossed the line first. She had succeeded in achieving the first part of the goal she had set herself six months previously.

Then, in October 2007, following a working honeymoon of cycling in the Canadian Rockies (yes, she is a little crazy), Morrison became the World Long Course duathlon champion and won by a convincing margin, more than three minutes ahead of her nearest rival. She had done it again. In fact, she had done it all. She was the best in Europe and the best in the world.

So what is left? What do you give to the girl who has everything? Or, in this case, how do you motivate the girl who has everything? Her answer is as simple as the concept of motivation itself.

'I am motivated to reach my full potential. I think that I have more to come, and I hope not to give up before then.'

Double Olympic sailing champion Shirley Robertson told *Be a Winner* about the I AM moments that shaped her destiny, taking her literally from the end of the breakfast table to the top of the medal table.

'I remember watching Mike McIntyre win a gold medal at the Olympics in 1988. He was Scottish and grew up in Helensburgh. I was sitting at my mum's breakfast table, with the little telly in the corner, and there it was – a 30-second clip of Mike winning his medal. At that time, they had just introduced an Olympic class for women, and I thought, "If Mike can do it, then I can, too!"

'I suppose that got me going. Then the real clarity came when I went to the Barcelona Games. Even when I shut my eyes today, I can remember watching the medal ceremony. I said to myself: the next time I come to the Games, I want to be the one standing in the middle of that podium singing my national anthem. I wanted it to be me. Before I wasn't so keen, there were always other things, like boys and college, always distractions, but from that moment I knew my path from then on.

'I worked really hard with the resources I had and went to Atlanta, the next Games, and finished fourth, just outside the medals. I was devastated. In some ways it meant too much. I worked too hard, I wanted it too much. In my sport, you have to be relaxed. I remember coming off the start line in my first race and my legs were shaking. I couldn't stop my legs shaking, I wanted that gold medal so much. It wasn't until after that, that I realised how I had to approach my sport. That's why in Sydney I approached it very differently, and won my first gold.'

And that's what a sharp dose of I AM is capable of achieving.

FOUR STEPS TO I AM . . .

- Find your inspiration and grab hold of it. Maybe it's a sporting hero on TV, your mum or dad, or just your love of sport. Whatever it is, use it to fuel your ambition.

- Set yourself targets. Start small, but always hit them. Let each target be your motivation, then aim higher each time.

- Enjoy yourself. Do what you are doing because you love it – and never forget that.

- Every time, try to be the best you can be – and reach your potential.

2

THE ABC-3D FORMULA

IN THE OPENING CHAPTER, WE SAW HOW CHRIS Hoy emerged to become a winner, but I AM is just the starting point. It isn't enough on its own. You can be motivated to play football on a Saturday afternoon or to go to the running club on a Tuesday night. But what happens when you walk into the changing-rooms? Is the motivation still there? Will you still feel the same halfway through a 10,000-metre run? When the rain is pelting your skin, your lips are chapping and the wind howls in your ears, will you still be up for it? How do you see the task through?

This is where the real effort starts, both mentally and physically. Having an idea or ambition is very different from actually achieving it – to getting faster, higher, stronger: the motto of the Olympic Games. Nothing happens overnight. You don't wake up on a Monday and by Saturday you are on the podium. So be prepared for some ups and downs. There will be good news and bad news.

First, the bad news . . . there are no short cuts. There is no such thing as the easy way if you really want to be the best you can be. However, the good news is . . . there are no short cuts! Because who wants to take short cuts anyway? A short cut is cheating; a short cut is taking the easy way out. It is cheating of the most futile kind, because taking a short cut is cheating yourself.

Scottish motor racing driver Dario Franchitti didn't win the Indycar

ALWAYS KEEP TRYING AND CHALLENGE YOURSELF, SAYS TONY HAWK

We're not here to talk up the merits of the PlayStation or the Xbox — we want you off the couch! However, Tony Hawk's *Pro Skater* and *Proving Ground* are two of the most popular console titles on the market today.

Yet while Tony's fame in Scotland is for his computer games, it must be remembered that he is a professional athlete — and one of the best in the world. He is the king of skateboarding and a pioneer. And he wasn't born with a skateboard glued to his feet. Nor did he pick one up and become instantly peerless. He applied himself to the task of getting good.

'I think that the most important aspect for me was to continue to challenge myself, no matter how far I got or how I rated in competition compared to others. As long as I could keep posing new challenges for myself and progress and evolve my skating,'

Series by taking short cuts, nor did jockey Willie Carson become British champion five times in 12 years by cutting corners. When Chris Paterson slots goal after goal after goal for Scotland on the rugby pitch, there is no one out there helping him. The ball isn't magnetically drawn to the posts. There are no short cuts that 67,000 Scotland fans at Murrayfield will accept.

There are many personal traits necessary to take your motivation from a thought to an action, a dream to reality. It takes guts, commitment, courage, endeavour and industriousness. To achieve your goals, it takes what we call the ABC-3D Formula.

That stands for Application, Belief, Competitiveness – Determination, Daring and Dedication.

APPLICATION: ESTABLISHING YOUR GOAL

Fittingly, at the beginning comes application – and we don't mean filling in a form! If you can become motivated to achieve a goal, be it to win a marathon or run for fun, then the next step to getting there is application. It is the act of paying close attention to your goal and putting in a constant, consistent effort to achieving it. It is about 'getting real' and taking it seriously. It is the starting point.

Tony told *Be a Winner*, when he was in St Petersburg in February 2008 for the Laureus World Sports Awards.

'Some people have visions of fame or fortune, but they never think that you have to keep working at it once you get there. In fact, you work more when you get there. So, for me, it was all about trying to come up with new things even though I was number one.

'I think that there were certain times that I just knew it was going to come together, because of how I was feeling that day or because I had truly prepared for whatever I was going to do. There were a couple of times when I really prepared well for big events, and I performed much better in doing that. I wasn't some crazy jock about it, but the fact that I did come in with some new stuff really helped me through it. In our sport, if you are going to compete in it, you've gotta be ready. People are always learning new stuff, and you've got to come up with new moves yourself.'

And, when it comes to application, there is no one who sets a better example than Roger Federer, arguably the best tennis player on the planet. The man who won Wimbledon at a canter for five consecutive years, 2003–07, the man who has been ranked at number one for over four years without slipping.

If you have seen Federer play, it is easy to be fooled into thinking that he has been simply blessed with sublime natural talent, that his consistency of class is down to pure ability. He is described as the 'matador' for the way he gracefully deflects shots back over the net, moving his snorting opponent from side to side while elegantly, almost arrogantly, flicking his wrists to produce match-winning shots.

But it wasn't just his talent that got him to where he is today. He was a talented youngster, but in his early days he wasn't even the best player in Switzerland, his home country, let alone the world. And he had many barriers in his way. He wasn't a great trainer, often preferring to laugh and joke around. He was too confident in his own ability and displayed a notoriously volatile temper when he lost a game.

When he was 16 he was ranked 60th in the world as a junior, and was often kicked off court for throwing tantrums (and his racket).

Yet one year later, he was world junior champion and five years after that he was a Wimbledon champion. How so?

The simple answer is that Federer finally started to realise that he needed to apply himself to his game, train harder and control his temper if he wanted to make it to the top. Federer employed a sports psychologist to help him curb the temper that had earned him the nickname 'Little Satan' as a child, and adopted a more disciplined approach to his training and game-play. Essentially, he 'got real'. He started taking his tennis, and himself, seriously.

In Scotland, we don't have a Roger Federer yet, but we do have two world-class tennis players who, some day, might emulate Federer. Both in their early twenties, the Murray boys, Andy and Jamie, are the future of Scottish – and British – tennis. Jamie became a Wimbledon mixed-doubles champion at just 21 – the same age that Federer won his first title at the same venue. Andy, meanwhile, broke into the world's top ten at 19, a year younger than Federer.

Much like Federer, the Murray boys were born with a natural aptitude for tennis, mainly due to their mother, Judy, herself a top player and coach. But it was the fact that the young brothers applied themselves to nurturing their talent at an early age that has helped them rise to stardom in one of the toughest sporting arenas in the world. And, as their mother recalls, it was against the odds in a country where tennis didn't enjoy much of a profile.

'It's probably taken the best part of ten years to develop them from promising eight year olds into world-class juniors who have the game to succeed at senior level,' says Judy Murray. 'As tennis is very much a minority sport in Scotland, there has not been as much support for developing world-class players as there has been for other sports, as you can't represent Scotland in tennis, only GB. Tennis doesn't tick the boxes.'

Like Federer, Andy and Jamie really started ramping up their efforts at around eight years old. Their talent was obvious, but Judy knew that talent was not enough. Application was important, even in their developmental years. In fact, especially in their developmental years, because it would provide a strong foundation for everything else that was to follow.

BEING SMALLER IS NO BARRIER TO SUCCESS, SAY BADMINTON STARS EMMA AND IMOGEN

Scottish badminton duo Emma Mason and Imogen Bankier are one of the top-ranked ladies' doubles pairs in Britain, and are in with a chance of representing the UK at the London Olympics in 2012. It has taken a lot of determination to get to this stage.

In a sport where the net stands 5 ft (1.52m) off the ground in the middle, height is a definite advantage. Neither Emma nor Imogen is particularly tall, and while they can admirably handle this setback now, when they were learning the game in their younger years, it was a severe disadvantage.

'It wasn't exactly easy sailing when I was younger,' admits Emma. 'The girls in my age group were very, very strong, and I was the weakest. Imogen and I were similar in terms of size and strength, but it never hindered the coaching I got. In fact, I think it was beneficial in some ways because it meant that we never got anything easy, we were never automatically number one. We both had to fight for things, and I think that's one of the reasons why we fight so hard now, because we had to when we were younger.'

'I think I was just determined,' adds Imogen. 'Because I liked badminton so much when I was young, I was just desperate to play all the time. Even when someone said to me, "You're too small", I still thought I was better than everyone. I just kept on going.'

'I think they were both born with a lot of natural ability,' says Judy. 'But it's been up to them to work hard to make the most of that talent. Andy is fortunate to be very well coordinated and very fast about the court. Jamie has great racket skills but doesn't move as well as Andy. He is also 6 ft 3 in. tall and left-handed, which is why his game is well suited to doubles.'

The example of Jamie Murray is a case in point when it comes to application. Realising that doubles was his niche, he worked at his game, as this was where he stood the greatest chance of success – which was proved beyond doubt when he became the first Brit in over 20 years to win a Wimbledon title.

Much of this has been down to Jamie taking responsibility for his career and employing a specialist doubles coach, Louis Cayer, to help develop his game. Much in the same way as Federer, Jamie addressed his game, brought in an expert and applied himself to the task.

'Since working with Louis, I have found a lot more direction in my tennis, and I realise what I have to do to get to the top. I know when I get on the practice court the drills and exercises I have to do to improve my game.'

Poignantly, though, Jamie says that the only way to actually make something of yourself is to apply yourself to being the best you can, reiterating the 'no short cuts' motto.

'I think if you have the self-belief that you can be a top player, and you work on the right things to better yourself, then you increase your chances of becoming successful. There are no guarantees of success, but you can give yourself the best chance of achieving it.'

This is only the beginning of the journey for the Murray brothers. It is still much easier for them to slip away than it is to keep climbing. Application is a trait that doesn't stop when you reach the top. If anything, it is only then that it really starts to come into its own. Ultimately, talent counts for nothing unless you apply yourself to making the most of it.

BELIEF: YOU KNOW YOU CAN REACH THE TOP

There isn't much to say about belief. It's simple really. You have to have it. It sounds tacky, but belief is something that comes from the inside, and nobody can influence that but you. You can't tell someone to believe that they can pass a driving test, get a job or achieve their dreams. They have to believe it themselves. But if they – if you – do believe, then, within reason, what you aspire to achieve is possible.

After motivation, after application, comes belief. That's what will take you to the very top, what will stay with you when the memories have long faded. When you said to yourself: 'I know I can do it.'

Ellen MacArthur is a believer beyond belief. She had the strength of mind to believe she could win the Vendée Globe – one of the longest, toughest races in the world. She set herself a goal of sailing around the world, on her own, faster than anyone else in history. But the Vendée Globe is more than just a test of physical and mental endurance. By taking on the challenge, MacArthur was placing her life in the great gaping jaws of the ocean, the most powerful and volatile force on earth.

Ellen had fallen in love with sailing at four years old when she went out on her Auntie Thea's boat. She had saved her school dinner money for eight years to buy her first vessel, an eight-foot dinghy called *Thr'penny Bit*. Ever since she was a child, she had been obsessed with becoming a sailor and worked hard to do so.

Navigating a yacht around the world on a solo mission in a race against time isn't a pleasure cruise or something to do as a hobby. It requires intense training, preparation, expertise and, above all, an absolutely unbreakable spirit. It is too tough a challenge for the weak-willed. MacArthur puts what she does into plain English for the novice sailor in her book, *Race Against Time*:

> Imagine driving a car, fast, off-road at night in lashing rain. You're forced to hang on to the steering wheel just to stay in your seat, and you have no idea what's coming next, as you have no headlights. To make matters worse, you have no windscreen wipers clearing your view. In fact, you have no windscreen. No roof. That's how it feels sailing fast in the Southern Ocean at night.

MacArthur, however, believed she could do it, while others doubted her. She sent out 2,500 letters searching for sponsorship and received only two replies. Maybe they didn't think it an event worth sponsoring or maybe they didn't believe she could do it. But Ellen believed.

When she eventually gained sponsorship from the Kingfisher organisation, this is what she said to her supporters in a letter when she decided she would take on the Vendée Globe:

> It is firmly cast in my own mind that I can do this . . . I am a tough cookie, not someone who gives up . . . I may sail alone out there, but without a committed team it could never happen. I can do this – just as we can do this. It is inside me to compete in the Vendée Globe . . . I will be on that finish line.

HOOP DREAMS: DARING AND SELF-BELIEF IN THE BASKETBALL WORLD

Taking a chance and trusting in yourself goes a long way in life. Take Scotland's basketball captain, Gareth Murray. Born in Arbroath, in Angus, he has experienced a life many young people can only dream about, but he had the guts to go out there and back himself.

Firstly, when he was just a teenager finishing up at high school, he decided to join the FLAG programme — Foreign Links Around the Globe — and travel to the United States.

'They helped me look for a host family and a high school to go to on an exchange programme, so I went there for a year, in Battle Creek, Michigan. That was pretty cool. When I was there I played football and basketball, because they run in two different seasons. So I played the year round.

'I then got offered the chance to go to a few colleges in the States. So I decided to go to a school called Kalamazoo Valley Community College. It was great. There is a huge difference in attitude. Coming from playing basketball in Scotland to playing in the States was so different. There isn't much interest here, but at my high school we had about 3,000 fans coming to our games — and that is a small school, of about 700 pupils. So to get 3,000 to every game is pretty amazing!

In 2001, Ellen became the youngest person and fastest woman ever to complete the race, out at sea for more than three months through ice and storms and snow – an amazing feat. Her faith had seen her through, a faith that she had from the very start, a faith that others couldn't see, or comprehend.

MacArthur went on to become the most successful female sailor in history. She circumnavigated the globe again in 2004–05, this time breaking Francis Joyon's record for a single-handed, non-stop navigation by travelling 27,354 nautical miles in 71 days, 14 hours, 18 minutes, 33 seconds.

When she was in the boat, alone, she famously recorded her feelings on a webcam. The world saw what she was putting herself through to achieve her goal, and although she was crumbling at the edges, her inner core of belief in herself remained strong as ever.

In one webcast from the southern oceans, she reported: 'I am running

'When I walked into town, people recognised me and asked how the basketball was going. It is just a totally different culture of sport. Everyone is really encouraging, you are in the newspapers every day — there are whole sections dedicated to high school sports. Basketball is just huge.

'I stayed there for two years and then decided to come home. I wasn't offered a full scholarship to cover my fees, and it is very expensive to go to college there.'

It was a bump back to earth for Gareth when he had to return to Scotland. But when he heard that the Scottish Rocks, the professional team that play in the British Basketball League (BBL), were looking for new players, he literally jumped at the chance.

'My friend told me about an open trial for the Scottish Rocks. To start off, I thought, I probably won't go, because it was in Glasgow. I was in Arbroath, so it was a long way! But then I decided, yeah, I will go.

'They had a pretty full roster already, as they were just about to start pre-season, but the coaches thought I had talent, that they should bring me on the team to see how I would do. So that was on a Wednesday, and by the Friday I was on the way to Norway for a pre-season tournament, and that was that!'

Three years on, and Gareth is one of the stars of the BBL and a Scottish international captain. And to think he almost stayed home because Glasgow was too far away!

close to empty. Physically I am exhausted, not just from the effort of sailing . . . but from the constant motion which makes even standing impossible. This trip has taken pretty much all I have, every last drop and ounce.'

Scotland's world champion hill runner, Angela Mudge, is an athlete who can share with MacArthur the difficulties of competing against nature, and also the belief that it takes to overcome adversity. Brought into the world in 1970, Mudge wasn't given much hope for a career in any sort of sport: she and her twin sister were both born with pedal defects, meaning that their feet were facing backwards. In her formative years, when she should have been running around and developing her legs, she was in plaster and braces. Learning to walk is an adventure for most infants. For Angela, it would be the biggest challenge of her young life.

'My feet were completely twisted, so my toes were facing where my heels were. My mum said they put them in plaster at one day old, and they had to stay like that for six weeks. Then they had to take them out for two weeks, then back in, gradually decreasing the time I was in plaster until I was two and a half. I didn't have an operation, as my parents didn't want it: it could have been unsuccessful. So I saw the podiatrist until I was about ten and had orthotic inserts in my shoes. I had to go to the podiatrist every six months or so, but it got less as I got older. I just remember walking up and down in front of somebody.'

Despite her initial, and indeed critical, disadvantage, from then on it was nothing but the fast lane for Mudge. As well as being educated to a doctorate level (at the universities of Leicester, Stirling and Edinburgh) by her mid-twenties, Mudge had advanced from being a track runner and cross-country racer (which she found too mundane!) to becoming a world-class fell, mountain and hill runner. She became a world champion for the first time in 2000, aged 30, and at 37 she won the toughest race in the world, the Everest Marathon, breaking the women's world record by 13 minutes.

'I don't think about my sport as demanding, I just go out and do it. You just see a challenge and say "I'm going to do it." And then you go and do it! I've always, from a young age, been in the mountains and enjoyed rough going, so to me, since I can run well on the flat and on the track, the natural progression is to put yourself to the test on the hill. What keeps me motivated is going to new races, new areas. You always know you are going to be in a beautiful place, so I pick races in places I haven't been to!'

Considering Mudge would once have been thought fortunate even to be able to walk, let alone become a world champion athlete, her achievements are a testament to her unflinching belief in her ability to succeed in her sport – and her life – no matter what the odds. In fact, like a true resourceful Scot, she uses her defect to her advantage, as she told *The Herald* newspaper in November 2007:

> I've got long tendons in my calf muscles. So you'll probably find that my ankle ligaments are stretched that little bit extra, too. When I go over on my ankles I very rarely tweak them. A lot of people

are very stiff in that area, so I think looser ankles are probably advantageous when you're running over that sort of ground!

COMPETITIVENESS: YOUR BURNING DESIRE TO WIN

C is for competitiveness. And to be competitive is summed up by a very simple saying. Something that sits at the forefront of the Winning Scotland Foundation's thinking: *Winning isn't everything, but wanting to win is.* That is competitiveness in a nutshell.

Those were the words of Vince Lombardi, the iconic National Football League coach who led the Green Bay Packers to five American Football championship titles in seven years from 1961 to 1967, including two Super Bowls.

But perhaps the most competitive man to have ever walked, or floated, is Sir Steve Redgrave. He has achieved so much for British sport, winning five consecutive Olympic golds from 1984 to 2000, an unrivalled phenomenon in endurance sport. Obviously, to be so committed to not just being there, but winning, Redgrave was (and still is) an intensely competitive man.

Aside from his Olympic success, he is perhaps best known for what he said to a TV journalist shortly after winning his fourth gold at the Atlanta Games in 1996. Almost demented by exhaustion, he unwittingly blurted, 'If anybody sees me near a boat again, they have my permission to shoot me. I've had enough.'

That was seconds after he had put his body through the most draining, agonising experience of his life. He had probably decided that being shot would be positively pleasant compared with what he was feeling. But by December of the same year, Redgrave was back on the water, ready to put in another four years of painful preparation for what was to be his last hurrah in Sydney. Why? Because he wanted the competition; he wanted to be out there, being the best. In his autobiography, *A Golden Age*, he said:

When I was younger I saw people approaching retirement after a really successful career and I'd think, 'Why are they giving up now?' I believe you should carry on until you're ready to retire. It's not always a question of quitting right at the top. If you enjoy it, carry on.

A COMPETITIVE INSTINCT GAVE ME THE COURAGE AND GUTS IN THE HIGH SEAS, SAYS SIR CHAY BLYTH

The year 1966 is best known for England winning the World Cup. Yet it is also the year when two young men — one from the Scottish Borders — embarked on a remarkable three-month sporting challenge. Chay Blyth, a 26-year-old Army sergeant from Hawick, and Captain John Ridgway rowed across the Atlantic in a boat the size of a large bathtub. It was a challenge not of skill or of talent but of sheer brawn and survival.

Bold and courageous, yes, but bordering on stupidity, especially considering Blyth had no seafaring background. But they were determined to do it. The challenge had arisen when a journalist named David Johnstone advertised for a crew to attempt the feat, but rather than join him, Ridgway wanted to take Johnstone on. It wasn't long before Blyth joined the captain on his mission. His reason was simple.

'We were just competitive people,' Blyth says. 'I would class it as more of an adventure, rather than a race. The race was more of a thrust to get us out there. I think it was initially "Let's race them", but because it was such an amazing thing, it was very much an adventure. We were going into the unknown, really, particularly for me, having no skills or experience whatsoever.'

Blyth and Ridgway had already been through a lot together in the Parachute Regiment, undergoing Arctic survival training in a snow-hole in Canada, and winning a 24-hour canoe race down the River Thames. This, however, was a test beyond the realms that either man had ever imagined. When they set off on 4 June, they were given a 5 per cent chance of surviving the expedition from Cape Cod in Boston across the ocean to Europe.

But these were two young men looking at things from an ABC 3-D perspective. They were full of determination, daring and dedication. And above all, they wanted to take on the challenge. They were to face hurricanes, tumultuous waves flooding their boat, perilous coastal rocks and near-starvation, but after 92 days of teamwork and drive, they prevailed, and were lifted by a rescue boat just a kilometre or so away from the Irish Aran islands, and became the first people of the 20th century to row across an ocean.

When Redgrave said he enjoyed it, that doesn't mean he actually enjoyed the torturous extremes he put his body through every day. He doesn't mean he enjoyed being sick to his very soul with nerves before a big race. He doesn't mean he enjoyed the overwhelming pressure of expectation placed upon him by the press and the public in the build-up to every Olympics for nearly 20 years. In fact, he says he physically hated the stress. But he had his own special way of dealing with it, of forgetting the pressure and expectation and savouring the moment he lived for: the competition.

'What I did was to visualise the race, picture ourselves and alongside us the Australian pair, whom we knew would be our principal rivals. Then I said to myself, "What are you going to do about it?" The answer was, of course, "There's no way I'm going to let them beat me."'

What Redgrave enjoyed was the feeling of winning. That's what he loved, and that's what gave him his competitive edge. He wanted to win, and that took precedence over anything and everything else. Being struck down with ulcerative colitis and diabetes didn't stop him. He wanted to be a winner, not just a participant.

There is another athlete who possesses competitive spirit in equal quantity to that of Redgrave: a footballer who has done for her sport in Scotland something to rival what Redgrave has done for rowing in Britain; a player who has scored more goals for her country than any other; a fighter; a warrior; a winner.

When Julie Fleeting first took to the field for the Scotland national team in 1996, the same year that Steve Redgrave was winning his fourth gold in Atlanta and requesting he be shot if he was seen on the water again, she was just 15 years old.

Little more than a decade later, in 2007, Fleeting enjoyed a pair of centuries with Scotland, amassing her 100th cap and, amazingly, notching her 100th goal.

She is one of Scotland's true champions and has been characterised by her unflinching competitiveness throughout her career, be that playing for Scotland, Ross County, US-based pro-team San Diego Spirit or her current club Arsenal Ladies, where she has won the European Cup. She refuses ever to let up, be it a World Cup qualifier or a game of backyard tennis – something her husband Colin discovered quite soon after he married her.

'He beat me at tennis once and that was it,' explains Fleeting. 'Just one game though – it wasn't even a set! It was on our honeymoon, and he will never beat me again. That's just what I'm like.'

And her husband isn't the only man to feel the tenacity of Fleeting. Julie trains on a weekly basis with Kilwinning Rangers Under-21 men's team. And though she admits her shortcomings in physicality, to her every session is another chance to prove herself.

'In training, I compete with them in many ways. I could never sprint past them if I were to do a 100m race, and in terms of strength the majority of them will be quite a bit stronger than me, but that's the kind of thing I need if I want to be better. There's no point in me going training with Under-13s, because I won't have them ahead of me to try and chase,' she says. 'I would never drop out in front of these boys. I wouldn't lose face. I would never give up. If they tell me to run, I will run, whether I finish at the front or the back. I don't care. I might not be at the front of their group, because I can't run as fast as them, but I will finish the run off.'

To be competitive is to make your opponents fear you, because they know you will not let them win, as international goalkeepers have discovered to their annoyance about Fleeting over 100 times.

DETERMINATION: NEVER ACCEPTING DEFEAT

D is for Determination. Determination is digging in. Determination is not quitting. Determination is knowing within yourself that no matter how tough things get, you will still be there at the end of it all. Determination is . . . Lance Armstrong.

Armstrong, from Austin, Texas, is walking (or cycling) proof that grit, persistence and an iron will can achieve anything, against any odds. From the very second he was diagnosed with testicular cancer, with multiple tumours eating their way up to his lungs and brain, Armstrong made a decision that would impact upon every second of his life, that would carry him through every obstacle he encountered.

In his second autobiography, *Every Second Counts*, Armstrong said:

> Before I was diagnosed, I was a slacker [he had been crowned
> world cycling champion three years earlier]. I was getting paid
> a lot of money for a job I didn't do 100 per cent, and that was
> more than just a shame – it was wrong. When I got sick, I told
> myself: if I get another chance, I'll do this right – and I'll work
> for something more than just myself.

This was the philosophy that carried Armstrong from a gaunt and
yellow-skinned cancer patient in 1996 to the all-conquering yellow-
jerseyed champion he is today, becoming the most successful Tour de
France cyclist of all time, winning the event seven times from 1999
to 2005. And that is no ride in the park. 'Le Tour' is among the most
gruelling physical and mental tests that a human being can endure.
Men have died mid-ride as they try to scale the vast mountains and
contend with the searing heat.

That Armstrong was given a 3 per cent chance of living through his
cancer, to simply survive is astonishing. To go on to win the Tour de
France seven times is beyond belief.

How did he do it? Like, really, HOW DID HE DO THAT?

It is a question that defies science. But Armstrong himself says he is
just a normal guy. 'Another bike geek from Austin' is how he describes
himself. But the answer is simple. He refused to quit. He would not lie
down for anyone or anything, be that an opponent, an Alp or a tumour.
He just would not be defeated. Armstrong is renowned as the greatest
road cyclist of all time. He has overcome considerable adversity to get
there. His determination to succeed, coupled with his never-say-die
attitude, ensured that even when his body was at its weakest ebb, he
could push through and beyond to prove himself as one of the most
physically tough and mentally strong men on the planet.

The term 'determination' is one that is often attributed to Scots.
As a nation, Scotland is proud of its reputation as a nation of
fighters, warriors, bravehearts. And that is an attribute that should
be fostered, because it is hard to come by. There are stories of great

Scottish athletes that parallel the inspirational determination of Lance Armstrong, many of which fittingly relate to endurance sports. When it comes to triumphing over adversity, though, this next guy tops them all, for he faced a challenge every bit as life-threatening as Armstrong's.

Graeme Obree is a Scot who has overcome what was very much a life-threatening condition to excel in his chosen sport. Above all else, he did it through sheer bloody-minded determination. Obree, who went on to become one of Scotland's most celebrated athletes and whose story has spawned a successful book and film starring an A-list cast, was a young man with severe emotional issues. He was bullied, depressed, suicidal and had an inferiority complex. Although a talented cyclist, he considered himself a worthless individual in a time when unemployment and poverty was rife in the west of Scotland. In 1985, he was at his lowest point. 'Less than zero in my own mind,' he wrote in his autobiography, *The Flying Scotsman*.

Having escaped with a suspended jail sentence for insurance fraud, Obree was a young man – just 19 – with a millstone of shame around his neck. After months of hiding out in his family home, in the spring of 1986 he went to his garden shed in a fit of tears and put a bottle of acetylene – a poisonous hydrocarbon liquid – to his lips. He tried to kill himself and survived only because his father arrived home early to find Graeme in a pool of his own vomit.

Why did he do it? Because he was, in his own words: 'filth', 'pathetic' and 'the social equivalent of a human appendix'. Yet, eight years later, Obree wasn't only a world champion and a world-record holder, he was the guy who had done it on a bike he had built in his workshop from bits of old washing machines. Competing against professionals with hi-tech equipment and expensive coaching, Obree was a true DIY man, achieving almost everything off his own back.

There was no significant turnaround. His life had improved for the better, but it wasn't as if he was snapped up and jet-propelled to glory. He had attended university, got married and enjoyed some success on the British cycling circuit. He was slowly and surely gaining more kudos as an athlete and more confidence as a result. Pushing himself continually harder, he became more and more prominent until, eventually, Obree's determination lifted him sufficiently far out of his hole to take on and conquer a truly astounding challenge.

He decided to face the toughest test of all. He wanted to break a world record. But not just any old record. It was what you could call an 'Armstrong-esque' record – the toughest of the tough: the Hour Record. This wasn't a race of one man against another. This was a man against himself. How far could he go on a bike in one hour? It was as paradoxically simple and difficult as that.

Obree went on to break that record – twice – travelling 51.596 kilometres in July 1993, and 52.713 kilometres in April 1994, becoming one of the most celebrated cyclists in the history of the sport. An insecure young man who used to fear walking into a bar in case he was looked at became one of the greatest sportsmen the world has ever known. How's that for determination?

DARING: FACING THE FEAR FACTOR

D stands for Daring, and daring is having the bravery to make a bold decision. Even the very best sportsmen and women in the world find themselves stuck in a rut sometimes, and they often have to take a gamble to get themselves out of it.

There are few braver (or better) sportsmen in the world today than Tiger Woods. Indeed, the name 'Tiger' was given to him as a mark of respect for his father's friend, a South Vietnamese soldier who was nicknamed Tiger for his valour and courage on the battlefield.

Tiger's story is littered with audacious moves, gutsy decisions and gritty triumphs, none more so, perhaps, than when he chose to risk his career and reputation – not once but twice – by altering his golf swing to improve his game. Woods would never settle for 'just OK', even if his 'just OK' happened to be the best in the world. Nope, his goal was to be better than that, better than himself, and that took daring – and courage. He knew that critics and cynics would speculate. He knew that, for a period, he might not play to the level expected of him, that he expected of himself. He knew that he might drop down the rankings, lose matches he would previously have won, and, perhaps worse, lose the respect of his peers for tinkering with a winning formula.

But he did it anyway. Daring? Or stupid?

Woods had enjoyed a record-shattering debut year in 1997, winning the US Masters by a ridiculous margin of 12 strokes, and rocketed up to world number one in only 42 weeks as a pro. But, as far as he was concerned, if he wanted to win on a consistent basis, changes

THE GREAT BATTLE IN THE POOL

One of the greatest gladiatorial battles in the swimming pool involved one of Scotland's all-time sporting heroes, David Wilkie. His adversary was John Hencken of the United States. Between 1972 and 1976, they raced against each other over 20 times, with Wilkie winning on nine occasions.

They were both outstanding swimming champions — but it was the head-to-head competition with Hencken that drove Wilkie to his greatest achievement. He became the first Briton in 68 years to take an Olympic swimming title when he won the 200m breaststroke at the Olympic Games in Montreal in 1976.

It was the exciting climax of years of hard work, toil and application in the pool — in training. Wilkie was covering 10,000 yards a day in two sessions in the pool, as well as doing muscle-building pulley and strength work. It was a classic case of determination and commitment to succeed at the highest level.

Wilkie also won two Olympic silver medals, two European and two Commonwealth Games titles, but his golden day in Montreal is still remembered as his greatest. On 24 July 1976, Wilkie of Great Britain took on the best in the world and demolished them in a new world-record time of 2 minutes 15.11 seconds, knocking more than three seconds off Hencken's old record. It was a fantastic achievement for the Scot.

Wilkie was actually born in Colombo, Ceylon (now Sri Lanka), in 1954, but his mother and father were from Aberdeenshire. As a youngster, he had shown promise swimming in the tropical heat of the Colombo Swimming Club, before coming to Edinburgh in 1965, aged 11. Then, as a Daniel Stewart's College schoolboy under the watchful eye of coach Frank Thomas at the Warrender Swimming Club, he reluctantly began to emerge as the greatest Scottish swimmer of his generation. It was his spell with coach Bill Diaz at the University of Miami that turned him into a world-beater.

Hencken, aged 22, had beaten Wilkie into second place in the 200m four years earlier would have to be made. He wasn't unbeatable, which meant there was room for improvement. Along with his long-time coach, Butch Harmon, Tiger went back to basics.

'We began by talking about it, asking ourselves, what do we need to do?' Harmon explained. Tiger was frustrated by his inability to control distance and trajectory on his shots when under pressure. 'I looked at tapes, saw that his clubface was shut at the top, and saw

at the 1972 Olympic Games in Munich. Now in Montreal, this was the moment of truth for two outstanding swimmers who had raced against each other in pools around the globe. Hencken, in lane three, was in good fettle. He had won the 100m breaststroke title in Montreal four days earlier in a world-record time. Wilkie was second.

That victory might have given Hencken the mental edge, but Wilkie knew he was stronger over a longer distance. Wilkie, also 22, was in lane four, and his heat time of 2 minutes 18.29 seconds was nearly three seconds faster than Hencken's. Also in the final were Nikolay Pankin, 27, and Arvidas Iouzaytis, 20, both of the Soviet Union, Graham Smith, 18, of Canada, Rick Colella, 24, and Charlie Keating, 20, of the United States of America, and Walter Kusch, 22, of West Germany. They were merely making up the numbers on this occasion.

Wilkie, with his trademark moustache, sideburns, white cap and goggles, cut a distinctive figure. The eight went off on the starting pistol, but it was a two-man duel between Hencken and the Scot. Wilkie took an early lead and turned up the heat. It was a blistering performance and as he came out after four lengths, he knew the medal was his for the taking. In front of 9,000 screaming and cheering fans in the Piscine Olympique, he kept pushing and pushing to ensure a new world record. The commentator declared as he finished: 'There is no doubt about the winner.'

So, four years after his tussle with Hencken in Munich, Wilkie had turned the tables, beating Hencken's record. His Olympic success was a unique mix of his upbringing in Ceylon, his early training in Edinburgh and his time spent at university in Miami.

He said in *Wilkie*, his biography: 'Swimming makes people very competitive . . . you have to be if you are to challenge everyone else. And it also reflects on everything else you do. I think I have become a much more competitive person since I went to America; they breed that into you there, for the whole way of life is very competitive, not just in sport but everything. Now I think it is lucky for me and my life that I have this determination to do well — which comes from swimming.'

that he was delofting a little coming into the ball, and was coming way too much from inside.'

Woods went to work on his technique. And his form, or certainly his win-rate, dipped considerably, and 1998 was dubbed the year of Tiger's 'slump'. But he wouldn't let that get to him. Yes, he lost a few games, won a few less. But, in his own eyes, his game was improving. In his own eyes, he was winning a more important battle.

'I think my ball flight's improved,' he told the press. 'I'm able to play in conditions I've never been able to play in before. An example was the British Open [held in Southport at the Royal Birkdale club]. The wind was howling. I know that the year prior to that there's no way I could have played that well.' (He finished third.)

It took until well into the 1999 season for Woods' body to finally 'click' with the new swing. He went on to enjoy the most successful period of his career. He accumulated eight wins in 1999, including the PGA Championship. In 2001, he achieved a Grand Slam – adding the US Masters title to the US Open, PGA Championship and British Open he had won in 2000. What's more, in 2008 he proved his daring again by winning the US Open with a serious knee injury.

That's what can be achieved by being brave and making a bold decision. But that's what is necessary sometimes. Sport revolves around taking risks – calculated ones – in a bid to garner success. Some of Scotland's finest athletes have undergone similar transitions. In 1997, Scottish rugby star Gregor Townsend had been riding on the crest of a wave. Having starred for the British and Irish Lions in the series win over world champions South Africa, he was one of the hottest properties in rugby. But by 1998, he was becoming frustrated with his game. Townsend said he needed to make a decision before his career began to stagnate.

'I found myself at a crossroads, with a big decision to make to save my rugby career. Although I had played stand-off for the Lions, the following season I was mainly playing at centre for both my club side, Northampton, and Scotland. My appearances in the No.10 jersey were few and far between and whenever I played there I was struggling to reach the standards I'd set the year before.

'With rugby union now fully professional, the game was evolving fast, and there were clear opportunities for me to become the best I could be. Playing at centre wasn't a problem in itself, but I believed that I had the ability to become a better stand-off than a centre. The latter was increasingly a position where physical power was more of a prerequisite than creativity. I was convinced my strengths were suited to the No. 10 jersey. Unfortunately, Northampton had England international Paul Grayson at stand-off and preferred to use me as a centre.

'I decided a radical change would increase my chances of playing stand-off more regularly, so I went to France and signed for Brive. As well as taking me out of my comfort zone, I felt the challenges of adapting to a new language and environment would bring out the best in me. It looked a daunting prospect – a back line full of internationals and a demanding coach meant I would have to play very well just to make the side.'

It was a courageous decision by Townsend. At the time, it was almost unheard of for a British player to move abroad, as the game had only been professional for three years. He would risk turning his life upside down and was putting his reputation and career on the line.

'However, after a couple of months of adjusting to French life, I revelled in the environment. I was selected at stand-off and also played there for Scotland in the Five Nations. I was in the form of my life – mainly because I was now playing regularly in the No.10 jersey – and helped Scotland become crowned the last-ever Five Nations champions. Our fantastic performances that year included a memorable 36–22 win over the French in Paris – something I felt a little bit guilty about, as my move to France had given me so much. Still, the French were happy that our win meant that we pipped England on points difference to win the championship!'

Townsend went on to become a legend in international circles, all because he took a gamble when he needed to.

DEDICATION: UNWAVERING COMMITMENT TO YOUR GOAL

If there is a path to achieving your goals without dedication, then we haven't found it yet. You can be motivated. You can apply yourself to the task. You can have buckets of belief and competitiveness, determination in droves and a downpour of daring. But unless you dedicate yourself, fully and unremittingly, you won't make it.

You might do well; you could enjoy some success. But you will not fulfil your potential unless you are relentlessly committed. And, worse, you will not look back upon your exploits, whatever they might be, with true satisfaction unless you can say you gave it your all. And that means utter dedication.

Britons, in general, are good at this. Not always blessed with the natural talent, or climate, to excel in sport, people from Britain have often clawed their way to the top through sheer devotion and endeavour. A classic example is perhaps the most famous sportsman on the planet, David Beckham. Despite the hype, and his transfer value, Beckham was never an outrageously talented footballer. His glamorous lifestyle is deceptive because many people don't realise how devoted he was to being first and foremost a top-class footballer.

Indeed, when collecting the runner-up prize for World Player of the Year on behalf of Beckham in 2000, former Manchester United legend George Best said of him: 'He [Beckham] cannot kick with his left foot, he cannot head a ball, he cannot tackle and he doesn't score many goals. Apart from that, he's all right.'

Yet there he was, voted the second-best player in the world. Beckham may have lacked all those skills, but he was unflinchingly dedicated to becoming a top footballer. He was one of the fittest players on the park, and the reason why he was so peerless when it came to crossing the ball and dead-ball striking was his commitment to practising.

Paula Radcliffe is another fine example of the dedicated athlete. There is no other way to become one of the world's greatest marathon runners. Her event is not one that anyone can do. There is no inter-changing. Most athletes can sprint 100 metres, dive into a pool or swipe a golf ball into the air. But only the specialists can run 26.2 miles. For someone to do it without practice, training and dedication isn't only impossible, it is downright dangerous.

So Radcliffe has dedicated her life to being the best and has had to come through considerable difficulty to get there. In the late 1990s, Paula was becoming aware of an obstacle that was hindering her greatly in her medal aspirations – her pace. Yes, even though she was one of the best runners in the world, she wasn't a natural speedster and was therefore pipped at the post by sprint finishers in races she had led from start to (almost) finish.

So, like any athlete with a will to win, she set to work on improving her sprinting. Second best was not good enough for Paula. Missing out on a World Championship gold in 1999 and an Olympic medal in 2000 by being too slow to finish was evidence enough, and by the time the World Cross Country Championships came about in 2001, she had developed her speed sufficiently to break away from her great rival, the Ethiopian Gete Wami, in the last 50 metres.

Radcliffe, writing about that race on her website, said: 'Every time I've dreamed of winning this title it's been with a sprint finish, because people keep telling me I haven't got one.'

She realised her dream because she was dedicated to achieving it.

But, of course, in Scotland we have our own athletes who can match, or better, anything that has been achieved by others. And, as you can imagine, dedication, commitment, devotion – call it what you want – is something that many great Scottish athletes will put their success down to. It is about going that extra mile to get what you desire, because you know that although it might hurt a bit now, it will be well worth it.

Scotland's great Olympic gold medallist Allan Wells, who won the 100m in the 1980 Moscow Games, was so dedicated that he even trained on his days off. And we don't mean a day he should have spent on the couch. No, Wells even trained when he was on holiday in Magaluf, Mallorca, with his wife, Margot (also an international sprinter) in 1976, at the request of his coach, Wilson Young.

'We had been given instructions on what to do,' Allan said. 'We found this football pitch, marked out a course, and we trained with trainers on. It was just a dirt pitch, the flattest one we could find. Then, towards the end of the holiday, a woman came walking across the pitch, and she pointed at me and said: "You're terrible, you've never let that woman beat you once."'

Wells was dedicated to winning, even against his wife. Margot was just as dedicated – in trying to beat him. The idea of not training was more alien to them than taking a holiday interspersed with some sprints. 'We were just mad – or perhaps stupid. You had to be so mentally focused on wanting to achieve something,' says Wells.

But that is what the ultimate aspiration for a great athlete is. To go to the Olympics or World Championships, and win. That is what the Application, Belief, Competitiveness – Determination, Daring and Dedication formula is all about. That is what they add up to.

We all have our own targets. Few of us will become world champions. But by following the ABC-3D approach, we can all become champions in our own field.

RECITING THE ABC-3D FORMULA . . .

- Application: pay attention to your goal, and don't stray from it. Focus all your efforts on that target.
- Belief: you can do it. You can do it. You will do it.
- Competitiveness: someone will always be standing in your way. If there wasn't competition we would all be champions. Tackle your obstacles head-on and go for the win.
- Determination: a winner never quits and a quitter never wins.
- Daring: it's OK to take calculated risks. Just think it through. It is sometimes necessary to suffer short-term hardship for long-term gain. Don't be scared if you know it's right.
- Dedication: commit yourself absolutely to achieving your goal. Don't make excuses. Don't slack off. There will be pain, sacrifice and disappointment, but it's worth it in the end.

3

TRAIN TO WIN

GET IN THE GROOVE FOR TRAINING

TRY THIS. **KICK . . . JUMP. KICK** . . . Jump. Kick. Kick. Kick . . . And again. Kick . . . Jump. Kick . . . Jump. Kick. Kick. Kick. There's a wonderful musical rhythm about this activity. Like playing a bass drum, a hip-hop dance or even an old playground skipping game. Rhythm and practice go together. And practice makes perfect. Now repeat that: practice makes perfect. And, again, practice makes perfect. Now do it faster: Kick. Jump. Kick. Jump. Kick. Kick. Kick.

We're going to look at the work you need to do before you can play your chosen game. Why a winner needs to approach the way they train in a consistent and logical way. Why they need to get into the rhythm and the groove. There is usually a nasty barrier to break through at first. Anyone who has had to put in hard work on any kind of training ground knows the truth about this. Basically, it's that awful physical feeling. You've been pushed to what you think is your absolute limit and you're exhausted.

'I am . . .' *pant* ' sooo . . .' *puff* 'unfit . . .' *wheeze*, you say to yourself. Well, so what? That's no excuse not to try. If anything, it should be an incentive. It's what you do about it that really matters, not how you are right now.

Your throat and lungs are stinging. You're trying to breathe through a painful stitch in your side. Your face is beetroot red and your hair matted with perspiration. It's this experience that switches off thousands of Scots. This alone is the temporary pain that stops Scotland's lumps of lard from getting off the couch and doing something for themselves.

When a sportsperson talks about 'hard work' – we can call this the sweat factor – they are referring to the sore bits. This is the exertion that hurts until you are able to build up a strength and resistance, and it is why training is so important, because it allows you to take part in a way that is far more enjoyable. In the early stages, though, it can be punishing.

BACK TO BASICS

Scottish footballers once used to face pre-season training sessions that were physically sickening. They still are in most cases. Even Gordon Strachan, the Celtic manager who won three consecutive SPL titles from 2006 to 2008, recalls his early days when footballers would return from their summer breaks after playing golf and lying on a sun bed and then face arduous long-distance slogs, sprints and hill runs that made many of them vomit.

He says the reason he was able to play football at a high level – the English Premiership no less – into his forties was not only his lack of serious injury, but also his inherent fitness from training at a very young age, running around the Edinburgh housing scheme where he was brought up.

It's the same at many rugby, hockey and athletics clubs, and in a host of other sports where fitness coaches put everyone through the same physical regime of near-torture. It happens in schools, too, in the sports halls where some over-enthusiastic gym teacher yells at his flabby charges as they huff and puff round a training circuit. Unfortunately, it often puts people off sport for ever – confining them to a life of increased risk of disease and ill-health.

But flat-out exertion is dangerous. Alistair Macfie, a senior physiotherapist at the National Stadium Sports Health & Injury Clinic at Hampden Park in Glasgow, who has been working with Scotland's youth footballers, says all athletes should learn to warm up properly before exerting themselves fully in their sport. He is particularly anxious to get this message through to the people who turn up late, perhaps minutes before a match, and then run out full pelt, kick a few balls and end up pulling a muscle.

'You can start your warm-up with some simple hopping, jumping, jogging and gently warming up your large muscle groups. This increases the body's temperature and increases the efficiency of your cardiovascular system – your heart and blood vessels – and allows the joints to be more lubricated and tendons and muscle fibre to be more supple. Then you can do some stretching of the main muscles to prevent strains.

'A proper 10–15-minute warm-up prevents injury. Your metabolism is more efficient, and the blood pumps more effectively. Muscle is a simple lump of meat that gets its messages from the brain. You need to get the blood pumping through your system to make it work effectively on any sports field.'

FIT OR QUIT?

There is a debate in Scotland about which sport produces the fittest athletes, but boxing and swimming are hard to beat. Alex Arthur is Scotland's super-featherweight champion of Europe and interim WBO champion, keeping up the proud tradition of great Scottish boxers such as Benny Lynch, Ken Buchanan, Jim Watt and Dick McTaggart. Alex goes through 12 three-minute training rounds in the ring, with a 30-second break after each round. His heart rate hits a maximum of 193 beats per minute. It was his father who devised some of the fiendish training and conditioning schedules to keep Alex in shape.

'I have to be very careful with my diet to keep my weight down, but you couldn't live at super-featherweight all the time. It's not possible, so you have to work your programme, building muscle and then slimming down in time for the fight. I'm very careful about what I eat.'

Alex was born and brought up in Dumbiedykes, in Edinburgh, in the shadow of Arthur's Seat, which has become part of his natural training ground. 'I've always been a Southsider. I have been out for a run on Arthur's Seat almost every day since I was 14 years old. I miss it if I'm away. I've invented some runs around the park that are lung-bursting.'

Scottish swimmer Gregor Tait, who won a double gold for Scotland at the Commonwealth Games in 2006, gives a hint of the commitment that is needed to train for his sport. 'A typical day would be up at 5.30 a.m., I am at the poolside at 6 a.m. Then from 6.15 a.m. until 8.45 a.m. we're training hard in the water. That's two and a half hours of swimming. Then at 9.30 a.m. it is down to the gym for at least an hour doing weight training or weight circuits. Then there is a rest period before being back at the pool for 3 p.m. We then go for a run, then back in the pool at 4 p.m. for another two-hour swimming session – then we get to go home.'

For Alex and Gregor, and so many other winners, there is a reason for all this 'torture'. And when you begin to accept it as a necessary part of becoming a winner, then you can start to handle the discomfort and appreciate that every incremental piece of training takes you nearer to your goal.

Gregor Tait says: 'I guess it's a case of "this is my job". But you can't cut corners to be the best . . . you have to put 100 per cent into everything you do.'

ATTITUDE COUNTS

But here we need to ensure that this expenditure of energy and effort is done in a proper and constructive way. Training really has to be geared towards your chosen activity – otherwise it is a wasted activity. And you need a coach who can inspire and instruct.

John Collins was one of Scotland's greatest football players, and he knows an immense amount about training professionals. In 2007, when he was coach of Hibernian Football Club, he changed the rules when it came to training – and upset some seasoned professionals. But Collins had experienced something special: he had worked as a professional athlete at the highest level, playing football for Monaco in the Champions League and living in France. And what he brought to Scotland is the Gallic attitude towards sport and its importance for individuals, for communities and for national wellbeing.

KEEP UP WHEN THE WORLD MOVES ON

Scottish 400m runner Brian Whittle knows a bit about planning. He made a specialised plan that would eventually take him to the Olympic Games in 1988.

'I remember in 1984, at the end of the season I had just come second in the Scottish Championships, running in 47.5 seconds. We reviewed the season, and by the end of the next I had made it to Scottish number one.

'My coach asked me my target, and I said the '88 Olympics. And he looked at me. Every athlete says that. He said, "Do you mean that?" And I said yes. I watched the guys in 1984 and I wanted to be part of it.

'He said, "OK, what time do you think you will have to run?" And we decided on 45.2 seconds.

'The reality was that I got within 2/100ths of a second of that time and made it to the '88 Olympics. I got on the plane to Seoul. And I ran my personal best (PB) at the Olympics. Unfortunately, I got blasted out in the semi-final. Even though I had made that target, the 400m world had moved on. The winner ran it in under 44 seconds. But things change, circumstances change, and you have to deal with that.'

France, the land of so many sporting greats, has kinder weather and excellent sporting facilities in every small town and village for both community and professional levels. But Collins wanted to show he could turn a group of good players into something much better and much stronger. He wanted his training sessions to be more effective – and his players to be more dedicated.

In Scotland, in recent years, we haven't always excelled at the dedication part on the training pitch. There's an element of national disappointment that we've produced capable sportspeople who have made a comfortable living out of professional sport yet haven't fulfilled their true potential.

Why is this? Partly because they have lacked the dedication to train hard and properly for their sport. Some of these players – often hailed and lauded by their fans – had an attitude problem. If they didn't get picked one week, they ended up in the pub, smoking cigarettes or going to the bookies, undoing all the work of the training ground. You'll still find one or two sportspeople like this in Scotland today.

In Scotland, we've cherished the wayward genius of sportsmen such as Jim Baxter of Rangers and Jimmy Johnstone of Celtic. These were footballers with such silky ball talents that they only needed to step out onto the pitch and perform. In 1967, Baxter, then with Sunderland, played a starring role in Scotland's famous 3–2 win over England at Wembley. England, at the time, were world champions after landing the World Cup in 1966 on home turf.

Baxter, niggled by England's glory when he felt the Scots were more naturally talented, wanted to show off his skill. He mesmerised England that afternoon. Denis Law opened the scoring with Bobby Lennox adding another. England fought back to level, before Jim McCalliog, an unknown Anglo-Scot who played for Sheffield Wednesday and was earning his first cap for Scotland, knocked in the winner. Few Scots would ever forget his name.

But Baxter was only ever capable of bursts of genius – and they became fewer and fewer after his Rangers years as his gregarious living and celebrity took over. He squandered his talent because he didn't bother much with training. His career was over by the age of 30 as he fell victim to a lifestyle of nightclubbing, heavy drinking and late-night gambling. One of the best footballers Scotland ever witnessed didn't have enough self-discipline to make his career last – and this perpetuated a Scottish myth that has lasted over 40 years: that Scots were inherently gifted and didn't have to bother training.

Thankfully, this generation is changing. People such as Chris Hoy, Andy Murray, Gregor Tait and Kirsty Balfour display the kind of characteristics that are required to succeed today.

John Collins says that talent is not enough. He's absolutely right. Talent only takes you so far. But then it has to be built on by hard work and practice on the training field. 'You can see those who give it their all and those who cruise along. I say to young players, "You've all got talent – but now you need to make the sacrifices. You're professionals. This is your chosen lifestyle so you should try to do your best at every training session and in every match,"' he said.

It's a point well made. And one that is repeated again and again by the likes of Sir Alex Ferguson, Frank Hadden and Walter Smith. If you're lucky enough to be a professional sportsperson, aren't you cheating yourself if you don't train as hard and as smart as you can? It's no coincidence that some of the greatest sportspeople today go back after training to practise again and again at an extra skill.

Think of Shunsuke Nakamura, the Japanese player who has been so successful with Celtic. He practises free-kicks after everyone else has gone home from training and that has made him a specialist – and a favourite with the fans.

Indeed, Nakamura's 92nd-minute trademark free-kick against Kilmarnock clinched the Scottish Premier League title for Celtic in 2006–07, and his remarkable 35-yard strike against Manchester United in November 2006 took them into the last 16 of the UEFA Champions League. All a tribute to Nakamura's extra time and dedication on the training pitch.

Every potential winner on the foothills of success needs help. A dedicated athlete or sportsperson cannot make the next level without a coach who can take them to a higher plain. As Olympic gold medallist Allan Wells said when talking about high-achieving winners: 'If somebody is going to start out with real potential, I'd say, "Go out and search for a coach who is getting results" – and I mean world-class results – in the event that you want to do. And see if they will take you on.

'It is important to develop the potential that you have. At least you have a chance of becoming what you want to become by doing that. It gives you a chance to develop that potential and that potential might be good enough to be a world champion – or an Olympic gold medallist,' he says.

It's not always easy to catch the eye of the best coaches. It might mean travelling some way to find them and pleading with them to assess your talent. Even over a short period, the great coach should be able to examine closely what you are doing, so that you can improve your techniques. Then they must be able to inspire you to do better.

Becky Merchant, one of Scotland's most promising hockey prospects aiming for the London Olympics, who won gold in the Australian Youth Olympics with Team GB, along with fellow Scots Nikki Kidd and Beijing Olympian Laura Bartlett, was prepared to move from Surrey to the east of Scotland, to play for Bonagrass Grove in Dundee. Becky was impressed with the coaching experience in Scotland: 'I find the coaching really good here. Dave Stott and Mike Gilbert are excellent. I find they are all individual. They are very good tactically. They will tell you to do something, and you go out on the pitch and do it and it will work. I think you need a coach that you have a lot of respect for, and then you just take on board every word they say. We do lots of different exercises. The coaches are very good at getting through lots of stuff in any one day to make sure that no one gets bored doing the same thing all the time.'

THE FOUR GOLDEN RULES OF TRAINING

On a flipchart at one Scottish Premier League football club, there are four words written on the board: *Explanation*, *Demonstration*, *Correction* and *Repetition*. These are nice and easy signposts on the way to becoming a winner.

ON EXPLANATION:

A good coach should be able to explain what you should be doing. He or she should be able to tell you clearly and simply how you can improve as an athlete. Your coach needs to work out how you learn, too. Is it more visual? Is it through demonstration? Or do you like the theory? We all learn in different ways, and a good coach should be able to help instinctively.

ON DEMONSTRATION:

Your coach should then be able to show you how you might be able to do it.

An amateur golfer with a handicap of six approached a young golfer on the practice range of an Edinburgh course. He'd watched the young lad slicing a few balls and wanted to offer some advice.

He told the young hopeful: 'I've wasted all those years on the golf practice range. For years and years, I've been hitting and hitting. I've read hundreds of books on golf. I wasn't getting any better and my handicap was about 14. Then I went to a golf professional who explained that the golf swing is one fluid stroke with a certain rhythm to it. He showed me. It's been a wake-up call. Even in my fifties, my golf has improved immeasurably – and so has my enjoyment.'

It shows that you are never too old to learn the proper way of doing something. Our veteran golfer added: 'Although it's tough to undo a lot of bad habits, I'm dedicated to changing the way I play. I've had to go backwards before I started improving again, but I'm getting there now.'

The key was the demonstration – in this case from a sensitive golf pro – on how to achieve something properly.

HOW A TOUGH TRAINING REGIME SEES BADMINTON STAR SUSAN HUGHES THROUGH THE WINTER

'At the start of November 2007, I took a good hard look at my position and decided that if there was any chance that I could make next year's Olympics then I had to get fitter, faster and stronger.

'So I sat down with Dan Travers [Scotland's High Performance coach], and a lot of other people at the Scottish Institute of Sport, and we looked at every aspect. As a result, I am in the middle of a two-month block of really tough training. And when I say tough, I really mean it. But I have to improve my physical condition.

'I've been aqua-jogging at Hampden – it's actually really good – and just working my socks off trying to get into really good shape for the start of 2008 and the final push for the Olympic selection.

'Over the winter, we have been doing quite a lot of outdoor training. It has been wet and freezing and I just want to stay in my bed. But it just comes down to how much you want to do it, and I say to myself that I bet all the other people in England and wherever else are doing it. Everyone has days where they can't be bothered. I have ideas in my head of who I want to beat, and I know they are getting up and training. Some days I really like going to training as well. I don't mind getting up early.'

ON CORRECTION:

This is a fundamental part of being a winner. There's no point in repeating something on the training ground that's wrong. This eventually becomes an instinctive bad habit. It's the duty of a good coach to point this out to you and help you correct it. Then it's back to dedication once again. It's back in your court.

And here it is important to make use of your mistakes. Mistakes are not to be dreaded – they are an important part of the improvement process. 'You can't learn new skills or behaviours that have any degrees of complexity without making mistakes along the way,' says Jim Thompson, founder of the Positive Coaching Alliance, writing in *The Double-Goal Coach.*

Thompson started the Positive Coaching Alliance in 1998. Based at the University of Stanford's Department of Athletics in California, it is now widely viewed as one of the most successful ways of inspiring young athletes to become winners.

'Learning is an active process. It's not a passive reaction. Learning happens when people are engaged and actively seeking. And the thing that most makes for passivity is fear of making mistakes.'

Thompson talks about ELM or *Effort, Learning* and *Mistakes.* He says acting like a winner involves three things:

1. Giving your best effort every time.

2. Continuing to learn to improve.

3. Don't let mistakes (or fear of making a mistake) stop you.

The Positive Coaching Alliance is winning new converts right across the sporting spectrum. It is the opposite of the old school of coaching, which is: 'win-at-all-costs'. It is about honouring the sport you play, respecting your opponents and developing to be a winner in your sport – and in life, too.

The ethos of the Positive Coaching Alliance has already been adopted in Scotland as a powerful cultural-change programme. Positive Coaching Scotland (PCS), launched by the Winning Scotland Foundation, has been endorsed by the likes of Scottish FA Chief

Executive Gordon Smith and 100-goal hero Julie Fleeting. It is a new way of encouraging young people to get involved in sport, rejecting the 'scoreboard mentality' of success and learning that true winning is an achievement gained through increased effort. The project is currently being rolled out among schools, clubs and wider communities across select areas of Scotland and is set to change forever how Scottish people view sport and its merits.

ON REPETITION:

This is when you need to get in the groove – to find that sense of inner rhythm in your training. Because once you have corrected the mistakes, then you have to start doing things properly. Every time. And practising this.

To learn this new, 'good' habit and make it stick in your brain you have to repeat it, repeat it and repeat it again and again. Do we have to repeat ourselves? Repetition is essential to becoming a winner.

And you can see how this has damaged Scotland on the world football stage. For a generation, Scotland has lagged behind other footballing nations because our talented players haven't worked hard enough on their core skills. Other European nations have surged ahead in technical terms. Yes, Scotland's national team has had passion aplenty and the fire to win, but this is not enough any longer. Young players in Scotland are now spending more time touching, tapping and juggling the ball in single sessions, in one-to-one sessions and in one-to-two sessions. Repetition and working on the core skills is the key to this. But there is also more work done on better coordination and drills that can enhance a player's skills.

Unfortunately, lagging behind in skills doesn't stop with our footballers. It has been endemic in Scottish rugby, too. Sean Lineen, an outstanding Scottish rugby player who now coaches the Glasgow Warriors professional team, was scathing about his new charges after a poor performance in 2007: 'I am worried about the shortage of tries, and we lacked a bit of punch, but the main thing is that the skill level is appalling. These guys are professional rugby players, and at the moment passing and catching seems to be beyond some of them. Poor decisions and our skill level doesn't match our ambition.' He's been working hard, with considerable success, to fix this.

Returning to football, John Collins again: 'In France, players have thousands and thousands of touches on the ball when they are youngsters. At the ages of nine and ten, they are working on the touch skills that become an essential part of their development.'

This breeds a more relaxed feeling about their ability when they are on the ball. John Collins tells his players to 'relax on the ball' but work like crazy to get it. Thankfully, this belief in developing skills is now being adopted in Scotland. Many believe that the large expanse of an 11-a-side pitch, even at its smallest dimensions, is still too big for children. When they are learning, kids spend too much time running around or standing still without ever touching the ball with their feet. This limits their ability to improve their passing and technical elements of the game. The fewer times that you touch the ball, the less chance you have of developing the basic skills that many other nations are concentrating on.

So, Scots have been at a disadvantage in the last few years. Our lower levels of skill, compared with other countries, has led to young people becoming disenchanted and eventually quitting the sport. A youth football study carried out in Scotland in 2003 pointed this out as a serious issue and recommended that all football for boys and girls under the age of 12 should be in small-sided games. Yet there are still examples today of eight, nine and ten year olds playing 11-a-side on full-size pitches.

The research was hardly rocket science but it is worthwhile. It validated a lot of thinking. For example, in a four-a-side game, the young players got more touches, had more shots at goal, gave the goalkeeper more work to do and made more passes.

So, according to the research, a specific and well-planned practice, training, competition and recovery regime is the only way to ensure optimum development of Scotland's sporting hopefuls. Programmes such as the Scottish FA's Fife Football Partnership have been implemented to achieve this. While kicking a ball or a tin can in the street was once the way to develop skills and build great teams, now it is simply part of Scotland's mythology and should be consigned to the rose-tinted history books.

THE ULTIMATE ATHLETE: Chris Hoy punches the air in celebration after his victory in the men's sprint final at the UCI Track Cycling World Championships in Manchester, March 2008. His specialist event, the kilo, had been scrapped after the 2004 Olympics, and once again he overcame adversity to win in a new event. (© Getty Images)

MOTIVATED BY SUCCESS: Triathlete Catriona Morrison flying the flag for Scotland at the Commonwealth Games in Manchester in 2002. She went on to become world and European duathlon champion in 2007, reaching the targets she had set herself a year earlier. (courtesy of Rob Eyton-Jones)

CREST OF A WAVE: Shirley Robertson, inspired by Scottish sailor Mike McIntyre while watching television at the breakfast table, greets her fans as she wins her first Olympic gold medal in Sydney, 2000. (© Getty Images)

FRENCH CONNECTION: John Collins believes the lessons he learned playing football in Monaco can be applied successfully in Scotland. (© Getty Images)

MUSCLE MAN: Andy Murray salutes his fans with a flex of the biceps after his sensational comeback against Frenchman Richard Gasquet at Wimbledon in 2008. It was a tribute to his fitness coach, who helped him reach peak physical condition to cope with the demands of a Grand Slam event. (© Getty Images)

CATCH ME IF YOU CAN: Scotland's record goal scorer Julie Fleeting puts much of her footballing success down to intense competitiveness and the hard work of her team-mates. (courtesy of Fraser Band, Scottish FA)

BRAVE NEW WORLD: Scotland rugby hero Gregor Townsend forced himself out of his comfort zone, moving to France to find a new direction in his career. (courtesy of David Gibson, Fotosport UK)

SCOTLAND'S GREATEST TEAM? The members of the Celtic side that won the European Cup in 1967 were all born within a few miles of Parkhead. Their achievement in beating Inter Milan 2–1 has never been equalled by a Scottish side. (© Getty Images)

TRAINED TO WIN: Allan Wells' desire to win was so strong that he even raced his wife Margot while on holiday in Mallorca in his bid to be victorious in the 100m at the 1980 Moscow Games. (© Getty Images)

SILVER LINING: Katherine Grainger (right) and her team-mate Cath Bishop train throughout the year just to be fit for a handful of events in the summer rowing season. Their Olympic medals are the reward for all the hard work. (© Getty Images)

MIXED MATCH: Jamie Murray enjoys winning the 2007 Wimbledon mixed doubles title with Jelena Jankovic. It represents over a decade of application to becoming a top-ranked tennis player, starting out as a promising eight year old. (© Getty Images)

MIND GAME: Britain's top female golfer Catriona Matthew, from North Berwick, believes that keeping a cool head when the game gets tough is the key to success. (© Getty Images)

CROWNING MOMENT: Gregor Tait can't quite believe it. He has just won Commonwealth gold in Melbourne, 2006. His victory was the product of one of the toughest training regimes in sport – and the Scottish team spirit! (courtesy of Bill Black, Scottish Swimming)

The Flying Scotsman: Track cyclist Graeme Obree overcame personal and mental difficulties to break the world record on a bike he had built from bits of old washing machines. (© Getty Images)

Shooting Stars: Susan Jackson (right) and Sheena Sharp show off their gold medals from the Melbourne Commonwealth Games in 2006. Susan's supreme mental focus on every single shot ensured she reached the ultimate target. (courtesy of Donald McIntosh, SSRA)

NUMBER ONE: Scottish racing legend Jim Clark, who won 25 Grands Prix and two Formula One championships, was an early pioneer of the T-CUP mentality – Thinking Correctly Under Pressure. (© Getty Images)

ARTHUR'S SEAT: Champion boxer Alex Arthur conducts a punishing daily training run through the south side of Edinburgh to keep his fitness levels up. His heartrate can reach 193 beats per minute when in action in the ring.
(© Getty Images)

FIRM BELIEF: European champion swimmer Kirsty Balfour is inspired by her Christian faith. She feels her incredible ability is a gift that she is destined to fulfil. (courtesy of Bill Black, Scottish Swimming)

TRIPLE CROWN: Celtic manager Gordon Strachan believes that his ability to play professionally into his forties came from a natural level of fitness he developed as an active youngster, playing in the streets near his home in Edinburgh every day. (courtesy of Celtic FC)

THE HARDWORKING REF IS A WINNER, TOO

Love them or hate them, referees, umpires and judges are an integral part of all sporting activities. Without them, sport in all its guises would be somewhat worse off, and in some cases, if there weren't someone there to take charge, many of our favourite pastimes would descend into little more than organised chaos.

William Collum is one of Scotland's top referees. At only 29, he has taken charge of some of the biggest fixtures on the Scottish Premier League fixture card — including matches involving both Rangers and Celtic — and is the youngest top-level official on the SFA's books. And, even though his role is only a part-time one, the responsibility that lies on his shoulders to keep 22 players and thousands of baying fans in control requires a lot of effort and commitment.

'Referees put in a lot of hard work,' explains William. 'It is not as simple as turning up on a Saturday, putting on a strip and blowing a whistle. There is much preparation required. As soon as you receive the appointment, early in the week, your preparation begins instantly.

'You also have to be very fit. I train six days out of seven, and most of these sessions range from road runs to track work and I also do training sessions on the football pitch itself. On average in an SPL match you would cover approximately ten kilometres.

'The SFA and UEFA are very supportive in this area. We use Polar heart rate monitors and all of our training data is analysed by sports scientists. We are given guides on fluid intake and general eating habits. I think all top referees can now be categorised as athletes in their own right. You are required to be very dedicated when it comes to training and fitness.'

Ultimately, sustained success comes from training and performing well over the long term rather than winning in the short term. All the signs are that there is no short cut to success in preparation. Scotland's over-emphasis on young people competing in the early stages of training and learning about their sport will only cause shortcomings in players' abilities later in their career. And that's not a way for Scotland to produce more winners.

And even if you've not quite made the grade and end up on the substitutes bench or as a reserve, then you've got to redouble your efforts and try even harder, so that you're ready when you get your chance to compete. We've been too indulgent in Scotland of the culture of the whinger who doesn't get a game. The great US college basketball coach John Wooden said that the fact that he could only pick five guys at any one time for a game meant that the players had to work harder to make the most of their chance.

Terry Butcher, the former Rangers and England player and now a Scottish coach, was giving out prizes to young professional footballers at a ceremony at Hampden Park a few seasons ago. He congratulated the lads on their achievements, but he said to them, 'You're only just starting out on your journey to become professional footballers. You've still got a long way to go and much to learn, and you have to be committed and dedicated to improving all the time.'

TRAINING TO WIN

For athletes preparing for an event such as the Olympics or a world championship, training is simply a way of life. They require what is known as 'periodised' training, aiming for peak performance at a point in the future. It can be a date with destiny.

Euan Burton is Scotland's top male judo player. He won European and World Championship bronze in 2007, and is one of the lucky few athletes being groomed for medal success at London 2012 on Sir Clive Woodward's podium programme. But that means a lot of hard work in the gym for Euan.

'The rowing sessions are gut-wrenchingly tough, but I get an almost perverse pleasure from pushing myself through the pain and hitting my targets. It always feels horrific at the time, but you get a great high once you're finished and you know you pushed as hard as possible,' he says.

Ronald Ross knows a thing or two about fitness, too. As a living (and still playing) legend of shinty, scoring 800 career goals, he says that to make it to the top of even an amateur sport like shinty, you must be prepared to work as hard as any paid athlete.

'The game has become more professional. Whereas some clubs were maybe getting by on one night's training a week a few years back, that is no longer possible, and clubs are training twice a week,' he points out.

'Kingussie [his club] set the standard and dominated the sport for 25 years, but more clubs are now following their approach having seen the success it brought. Clubs are now more focused on what it takes to get to the top. You have to be brave and very fit. I think the athletes at the highest level in shinty are as fit as Premier League footballers.'

Katherine Grainger is one of Scotland's greatest rowers with two Olympic silver medals, in 2000 and 2004, and four world championship gold medals. All of her races take place between May and August.

'Yes, we are one of the slightly unfortunate sports,' she says. 'We train every month of the year, and all our racing happens in a short competition period in the summers. The majority of the year it's just training, and we don't compete during the winter. We have about four major internationals a year and one of those is the top priority, and then there is the Olympics in Beijing.'

So how does she motivate herself in training when competitions are months away?

'It's probably one of the hardest areas of our sport, and training itself is very intense and hard work. We are out in the snow, wind, rain and darkness a lot of the year. Mentally, it's really tough and takes its toll physically. But there's no need for extra motivation in an Olympic year.

'Hard work is what you buy into at the beginning and that's what is going to take you to the top. I've done enough of it for years to know what it is like. You have to build steps to the big-time goals and work on short-term goals each week with something to aim for and look forward to. You just have to break it down and make it more manageable.'

Grainger doesn't usually get rest days. She has rest times. If she isn't training, she is chilling out, because there is as much chance she will burn out from under-resting as from doing too much.

'Rest is actually part of the training, and if we mess up the rest time it's almost just as bad as overtraining. If you train seven days a week you make sure any down time that you have is very much down time. You learn to be very good at time management!'

WHEN WORLD CUP FRENZY WENT TO SCOTLAND'S HEAD

Prior to the 1978 World Cup, with the vintage of Kenny Dalglish, Graeme Souness and Joe Jordan in his ranks, Scotland manager Ally McLeod had secured the country's eternal affections after leading his team to a 2–1 win over England at Wembley in 1977. When Scotland then went on to qualify for the World Cup in Argentina by beating Wales 2–0 at Anfield, the hype and hope that was pinned on McLeod and his boys was nearing delirium. The country had worked itself into a frenzy of excitement and anticipation that this could be Scotland's World Cup.

McLeod, an ebullient character, revelled in the euphoria. He expected Scotland to go all the way in the competition, and wasn't shy in sharing his optimism with the public. When asked what he would do after the World Cup, he (over)confidently responded, 'Retain it.' The players, meanwhile, were waved off to Argentina in fanfare fashion, being paraded around Hampden in an open-topped bus — an exercise usually reserved for teams who have won something.

Of course, not everyone is a young star in the making. The footballer Craig Brewster is a classic 'late developer'. Some meteoric careers are burned out long before this steely Dundonian striker got into his goal-scoring stride. He was 26 when he signed as a full-time professional footballer with Dundee United. It meant so much to him, playing for the team he had supported since boyhood, that he relished every single moment and when he arrived at training each morning it was a 'punch-me-I'm-dreaming' moment.

'I've been a full-time professional footballer for 15 years now. I turned 40 in December 2006 and staying in good shape is the key for me. I'm still extremely fit. I've never had pace, but my general fitness allows me to keep up with the rest of the guys,' he explains.

'There is one thing that is important. That's enthusiasm. This is a major factor for me still playing late on in my career. But there is no getting away from the fact that you have to put in a lot of hard work.'

He recalls his early days as a pro: 'I'd been playing senior football since I was 18 and suddenly I was a full-time player. It wasn't a chore.

Unfortunately, the Scots had forgotten about the application that took them there in the first place. And the ignominy was quick to follow. An unexpected — but not altogether surprising — defeat by Peru and a barely deserved draw with Iran were compounded by Willie Johnston being sent home for failing a post-match drugs test. McLeod and the Scotland squad were in tatters. All of a sudden, Scotland were up against it.

When just one week earlier they had been much fancied, the Scots now faced a crunch play-off against the 'total football' of the Netherlands to progress beyond the first round of the World Cup.

And, in typical Scottish fashion, now that they were up against it rather than being the favourites, they began to perform again. Free from the pressure of expectation, the Scots were on fire, showing the dazzling form that took them to the World Cup in the first place, epitomised by Archie Gemmill's iconic strike after bamboozling two Dutch defenders inside the penalty area. Scotland eventually won 3–2, but needed to win by four clear goals to qualify for the next stage. Once again the term 'glorious failure' was stamped across their copybook as they made the long trip back to Scotland. They were kicking themselves instead of the ball.

I don't have to drive an hour there and back for training three times a week in the middle of winter, getting home at 10.30 at night. Suddenly, it was my full-time job. It was a massive change. Unlike some younger guys who come straight out of school and don't really know what they've got until it's too late, I really appreciated what I had,' he says.

This sporting opportunity has had an immense impact on a player who had taken a series of jobs as a builder, cement-mixer driver, waste-disposal truck driver and even a sports-shop owner. More than anything, Brewster wanted to play top-level football.

Brewster is a straight talker when it comes to training. 'Some people just expect things to happen when they step out on a football pitch. But without the hard work, you won't get to the top. Of course, sometimes you might get lucky. But if you stay in good shape, you have the chance of playing to your potential – and playing longer.'

| **TRAINING TO WIN MEANS REMEMBERING THESE STEPS . . .** |

- Practice makes perfect: if you do it enough, you will master it. Remember: Explanation, Demonstration, Correction and Repetition.
- The sweat factor: hard work is necessary – there are no short cuts. It hurts, but your reward will come later if you put in the work now.
- Don't waste your gifts: pure talent is not enough. Work to develop that talent by having the right attitude. Every top sportsman and woman in the world will tell you that.

THE MARK OF A TRUE SPORTSMAN

There is no doubt that, as far as role models go, Andy Murray is an example for all of Scotland.

The heart, skill and determination that took him to a Wimbledon quarter-final in 2008 is precisely the kind of attitude that everyone should aspire to have. As Hugh MacDonald of *The Herald* pointed out, his performance against the eventual champion Rafael Nadal showed what a credit he is to Scotland:

'Murray has the best of the Scottish psyche and has no truck with the worst. If pessimism and self-destructiveness was an Olympic sport, Scotland would once have monopolised the gold medal. But there is a new generation and Murray is its standard-bearer . . . [he] has been shamefully portrayed as a dour Scot in newspapers that regularly and properly rail against racist stereotyping. He is always moaning, they say. The reality is he does not whinge at outside factors. He reserves the strongest criticism for himself.

'The same newspapers then swivel on an axis to criticise Murray for being too self-confident. He is too sunny about his prospects, they claim. So now we have a dour, pessimistic Scot with a bright-eyed, hopelessly romantic view of his future.

'The English press and many tennis supporters south of the border may not "get" Andy Murray. Gloriously, Scotland does. And we have him to keep. Wimbledon 2008 is just another step to greatness for a remarkable young man.'

4

MENTAL WEALTH – WHAT IS SPORTING INTELLIGENCE?

THINKING ABOUT THINKING

HERE'S A BRAINTEASER. SEE IF YOU CAN WRAP your head around it. Is it possible to think without thinking? As in, can you be thinking without realising it? Well, without delving into our subconscious too far, the answer is that we all 'think' without 'thinking about it'. We are using our brains every second of the day without actually realising it. This chapter is about thinking about how you think.

Imagine playing a game of football, basketball or hockey. Read the next paragraph and look at the number of actions your brain must execute in a matter of seconds.

Remembering what your coach said about a weakness in the opposing team's defence (*verbal memory*), you decide to take the ball up the right side of the field instead of going through the middle (*executive functions or planning*). Suddenly, an opponent nips in and steals the ball from you. Reacting quickly (*reaction time*), you recapture it. From a previous glimpse of the right area of the field (*spatial memory*), you recall that it is now too well covered by the defence for you to advance any more. So, rather than going right, you alter your strategy towards evasion (*'gear changing'* or *cognitive flexibility*). When an opening finally appears, you cut through to the right and hammer the ball into the net (*hand–eye coordination*).

Your brain has to process six different actions in just a few seconds of play! Now imagine how much you need to use your brain in a whole match or race. It is simply impossible to perform in sport without thinking. So if you can 'think about how you think', and even train yourself to think in a different way, imagine the impact it could have on your performance.

When Celtic legend John Clark took to the field to play for Scotland against Brazil in 1966, he had a lot to think about. Running out for your country is a lot of pressure on anyone's shoulders, but to do it against the world champions obviously makes the challenge even greater. But he knew he could cut it with the best of them. So on that day, that was exactly what he did, cutting it with the best there has ever been.

'The Brazil team featured Pelé – he was the king,' recalls the Lisbon Lion. 'The fact I was playing against him almost took my mind off the game, but I managed to stay focused and we drew 1–1,' he recalls.

The moral is that performing in sport is all in the mind, even at the top level. Clark – known as 'the Brush' for his role as a defensive sweeper – might have been overawed by the great Brazilian, but he kept his head and concentrated on the job at hand, as did his Scotland team against a nation who won the World Cup three times in four attempts in that same era. In 1967, that same Scotland team went on to beat the new world champions, England.

People don't just become world or Olympic champions because they can run, cycle or swim faster than their rivals over a certain distance. They have something else over their opponents, because the most powerful piece of kit these winners possess doesn't stay in their locker or their holdall. It stays inside them. What sets them apart from the rest is that they have the right mindset and can call upon their winning mentality when it is demanded of them. The most powerful piece of kit they own is their brain, because they can use it to edge them to victory.

SPEED OF THOUGHT

If all of Scotland's motor sports winners were gathered at Knockhill, it would be an illustrious starting grid — and the race of the century.

From Ron Flockhart and Allan McNish — both Formula One drivers but better known as two-time winners of the gruelling Le Mans 24 Hours race — through to Dario Franchitti, the 2007 Indycar champion, the line-up of greats would be a mouth-watering prospect.

Of course, there would be tremendous rivalry between two Scottish legends, Jim Clark from Duns, world champion in 1963 and 1965, who won 25 Formula One Grands Prix from 72 starts, but who sadly died in 1968, to Sir Jackie Stewart, who surpassed Clark's achievement, winning three Formula One titles and a host of other motor races. Jackie drove for BRM then left to drive for Ken Tyrrell. Twenty-five of his 27 wins were for Tyrrell, including all three of his World Championships in 1969, 1971 and 1973. In the decade from 1963 to 1973, the two Scots won half of the World Championships, an amazing record of winning.

Just behind on the grid would be recently retired driving ace David Coulthard, from Twynholm, who has narrowly failed to win the ultimate prize of F1 world champion, but has finished runner-up in 2001, and third three times, notching up 13 Grand Prix wins. Alongside would be Bathgate boy Dario Franchitti. He began racing karts in 1984 at 11, landing his first crown in the Scottish Junior Kart Championship. He competed and won in the British Formula 3 Championship in 1994 and the FIA International and German Touring Car Championships in 1995–96 before making the move to CART in 1997. Dario won the Indianapolis 500 at the Indianapolis Motor Speedway in May 2007.

Among the giants would be former world rally driving champion Colin McRae, killed in a helicopter crash just 200 yards from his home in 2007. Colin is sadly missed by motorsports fans and he became the first British driver to win the World Rally Championship, and the youngest winner, when he took the title in 1995. Also in the line-up would be Colin's father, Jimmy, five-times UK rally champion.

Every one of those inspiring motorsport competitors shares a common trait — speed of thought and action made them winners. The reactions needed to win are honed on the track in the heat of intense competition. Whether it was purely instinctive, or learned, they all knew how to think and then act correctly under pressure. Professional motor racing also requires immense courage to cope with surviving the terrifying spills that have claimed so many lives.

TRAIN YOUR MIND

Commonwealth champion rifle shooter Susan Jackson hones her concentration to get in the zone when it matters.

'When I'm preparing for a competition, I work on shutting out all the things that are going on round about me on the range and just focus on me, my gun and the 60 shots that are ahead of me. I do this by sitting behind my firing point and watching the wind flags, thinking about what conditions I will try to shoot in.

'This ability to concentrate on one simple thing allows me to shut out all the other distractions that might be happening around about me — other shooters getting ready, spectators making a noise, range officers and officials wandering up and down the firing point.

'I generally get nervous before a big competition, but I need to keep my heart rate down and keep control of the adrenalin to shoot well, so I work hard on keeping calm and thinking positively about my shooting. I have a very clear internal image of me firing a good shot in any of my three positions and I use this strong imagery to try to control the excitement and keep calm, but at the same time maintaining real positivity and belief that every shot can be a good one.'

As John Clark testifies, he puts down his shackling of the great Pelé to being able to stay 'focused', not to being a better player than him. You can be the greatest talent to have walked the earth, but if you don't use your brains, you will struggle to make it to the top.

And when we say brains, we don't mean classroom smarts or exam aptitude. We mean 'sporting intelligence'. Athletes with sporting intelligence have the mental capacity to cope with all the pressures, crises, distractions and variables that can affect even the tiniest fraction of their performance. That is often the difference between winning and losing – and the level of that sporting intelligence is what gives winners that extra few per cent when it really matters.

In any environment in sport, be that the snooker table or the Champions League arena, mental composure is essential in separating the best from the rest. In so many contests, it is difficult to distinguish who will win on paper. Rangers or Celtic? Hendry or Higgins? Murray or Murray?

If a contest is so evenly matched when it comes to technical prowess and physical skill, it is the competitor with the will to win who will walk away with the prize. So let's talk about some of the ways in which Scottish athletes have capitalised on their sporting intelligence.

FLICKING THE SWITCH – WHEN DOES THE MIND TAKE OVER FROM THE BODY?

If you use your brain in the right way, it can be the most deadly weapon in your arsenal, regardless of how fit, fast or strong you are. Because, at some point or another, you are going to come up against someone who is just as fit, fast or strong as you. And how are you going to win then?

All of Scotland's great athletes know this. And so do their coaches. They know that for them to stand a chance of winning on the world stage, they don't only have to out-perform their opponents, they have to out-think them, too.

Tennis is an archetypal example of where sporting intelligence comes into play. It is a sport that requires flawless technical skill and a supreme level of fitness and flexibility, but it is also a psychological duel with your opponent. Every point is a battle of minds.

You look into your rival's eyes across the net. You are thinking, how will I return the serve? Will I come up to the net or play a long game? They are thinking about you, too. Will he go for power or accuracy in the serve? Is she squeaking her shoe on purpose every time I serve, to put me off? There is so much to think about beyond getting the ball over the net.

Joanna Henderson is one of Scotland's great tennis prospects for the future. Still in her early teens, she has dominated her age group in British tennis for several years now. However, she already realises the importance of mental strength to complement physical prowess in her chosen sport.

'You have to be very mentally strong to carry yourself through a lot of matches – you can't just do it on physical ability alone. In fact, it's mostly mental. I just love being competitive, going one on one with someone else. You just have to want it enough.'

WARRIORS DON'T NEED TO BE WOUND UP FOR BATTLE

The Scots have a proud legacy of being great warriors. From William Wallace to the Black Watch, we have produced some truly noble fighters. Yehuda Shinar, the Israeli winning expert, says there is warrior spirit in nearly all of us. It's just about finding it within you.

'A warrior doesn't need you to tell him to give 110 per cent. They are never satisfied. They are the kind of people that when they finish a game where they did well, five minutes later they will be sitting down thinking: "What could I have done better?" That is their mindset. That's why they are always improving. They will have a very high threshold for pain, physically and mentally.

'In this regard, there are three types of people: there are those who are "born warriors"; those who will never be warriors, because they don't want to be; and there are those who become warriors, when they discover the warrior within them. The last category accounts for the vast majority of people.'

Yehuda doesn't regard a warrior as a blood-and-thunder, do-or-die kind of person. They are more thoughtful than that. They think about the mistakes they make and try

And if Henderson is a star of the future, then Andy Murray is very much a Scottish hero of the hour. One of the best players in the world, Murray knows better than most how important the right mentality can be.

'At the top level, it's really important to be able to analyse what's going on during a match and to be able to employ tactics and patterns of play that will upset your opponent's game – finding a way to win, whatever the circumstances,' he says.

Andy Murray likens a game of tennis to a boxing match, because he doesn't only have to take on his opponent physically, there is also a mental duel going on. He is constantly probing his rivals to see where they may let their guard down.

'You need to be very strong mentally to get to the very top and to stay there. You need to have a good tactical brain and be able to solve your own problems. Every point is a problem to solve! I am lucky enough to be strong tactically and to have a lot of variation in my game. I like working out an opponent's weaknesses and exploiting them. That's why I also like to follow boxing.'

to come back and be better. There are lots of 'warriors' like this in Scotland, people who are tough and abrasive, but measured and clinical, as well.

Take Graeme Dyce. He is a warrior all right. The Edinburgh-born teenager is hot on the heels of Andy and Jamie Murray in becoming the next big thing in British tennis, highlighted by his winning the men's doubles at the Junior Australian Open in January 2007. There are so many reasons to label Graeme with the 'warrior' tag, not least because his nickname is 'Wallace', after William, because of his fiery red hair.

He was also labelled a 'street fighter' by legendary tennis coach Nick Bollettieri. Graeme spent one year training at Bollettieri's world-famous training academy in Florida, where the likes of Andre Agassi and Maria Sharapova learned their trade. That's where his inner warrior came to the fore.

'When I first got there I had to start at the very, very bottom,' explains Graeme. 'When you get there they don't care about your ranking, you need to prove yourself. So for the first couple of months I nearly killed myself and really went for it, just to get up there. I kept at it because I knew if I could get up there it would be worth it.'

To find your true mental wealth, first you should seek out your inner warrior.

And when Murray talks about exploiting weaknesses, this also means he has to work on his own flaws as well. Ever since he burst onto the scene as a floppy-haired teenager in 2005, Murray has been lauded as one of the most naturally gifted tennis players in the game. But he isn't perfect. When he does suffer a defeat, he makes a note of his weaknesses and works hard to develop them into strengths. One such example of his determination to work on his failings was after he lost in the first round of the Australian Open in early 2008 – an event for which he was seeded ninth. He put his loss down to 'a bit of inexperience' and then said, 'The more Grand Slams I play and the more big matches I play, the more I'll learn from them and won't make the mistakes that I did in this match.' He proved his own point by reaching the quarter-finals of Wimbledon for the first time in 2008.

PERFORMANCE UNDER PRESSURE: COPING . . . NOT CHOKING

Performing under pressure is one of the most vital components of sporting intelligence, as Andy Murray tells us, having been placed under so much pressure at such an early stage in his career. Performance under pressure is about dealing with the adrenalin hormone that surges through your bloodstream as you await 'go time' in an event. It is making the right decision in a split second. It is coping with the expectation placed on you by others. Any one of these aspects can make an individual crumble. To have them towered on top of one another is nothing short of terrifying.

Coping with pressure is a tough thing to do. Even the best athletes in the world struggle with it – such as Gavin Hastings, when he missed a pressure kick against England in the 1991 World Cup semi-final. But that was just a one-off. Hastings, in general, was a master of coping with pressure.

'Yes, there was always pressure, but you just deal with it. You don't necessarily think about it. You can worry about it before the game, but it's just a matter of going out onto the field and doing it. I didn't get too bogged down by it, and if I did miss a kick or a penalty, I wouldn't let that affect the rest of my game,' says Hastings.

'My take on pressure was that I would rather have me doing it than somebody else, because I was confident in my own ability: I felt that I was better able to handle that pressure than anybody else, just because of the type of person I was. I would much rather be in control of the situation.

'Adrenalin is a very powerful thing, if you learn how to control it. You shouldn't be scared of it either, as it is a very positive thing. Coming from experience, you realise it is part and parcel of the game.'

Gavin not only thrived on pressure, he also had a sure-fire method of getting over disappointment.

'My mentality would be to go train a lot harder and practise my goal kicking. Hasn't everybody who has come back to have success after a tough time said, "I trained hard" or "I worked hard on my game"?

'In 1985, I was captaining Cambridge University in the varsity match. We were overwhelming favourites to win, and I had a shocker. We lost 7–6. I missed a few kicks and got tap tackled a few yards from the line. This was the second Tuesday in December. I played two more games in the next three weeks and trained a lot. I played very well in those games, the second of which was the national trial. Two weeks later, I got my first cap for Scotland. I kicked six penalty goals, and we won the match. That is a prime example, to go from losing in front of 40,000 people at Twickenham to six weeks later winning your first cap!'

CONCENTRATION, CONCENTRATION, CONCENTRATION ...

Coping under pressure is achievable, and controllable. And it comes down to two key thought processes that encapsulate performance in any field: *Concentration* and *Confidence*.

A PRECISE ROUTINE IS HELPING SPRINTER LIBBY CLEGG

Libby Clegg is one of Scotland's premier young sprinters, and is a hot tip to win medals at the Paralympics. She has Stargardt's Macular Dystrophy, causing her vision to be limited to the corner of her left eye. And although she has only sprinted competitively for a couple of years, she has already won gold (100m and 200m) at the British Open and silver (200m) at the IPC (International Paralympic Committee) Athletics World Championships, meaning she is quite literally one of the fastest disabled athletes on the planet.

Libby has a very precise routine that she goes through every time she lines up for a race. It is her way of getting 'into the zone', making sure her mental focus is right before the gun fires. Just don't get in her way when she's doing it ...

'I just try to concentrate on what I am doing, though I do tend to get in really bad moods before a race,' warns Libby. 'If someone starts pestering me about how I should be warming up, I don't like it. You'll get a mouthful. My mum gets it, my coach gets it, or my guide, Lincoln, gets it. I don't like to be spoken to. The worst question is, "How are you going to run this race?" Don't ask me! I don't know how I am going to run it, and if you start talking to me about it, it will wind me up.

'I like to do my own thing. I like to warm up by myself. I like to sort my shoes out and make sure my kit is all sorted by myself. I start my warm up at least an hour before, just so I can roll into it. I like to prepare in my own time with no one speaking to me, unless it's important. I don't like to know who my competition is. In a big competition, I don't want to know who is in my heat. I would rather not worry about it, and I can be more relaxed. If I don't know who it is then I will automatically go into the race thinking I will just have to do my best run and best time.'

When it comes to concentration, there are few sports in the world that require more focus than rifle shooting. Take Susan Jackson, Scotland's gold medal winner at the 2006 Commonwealth Games. Jackson, alongside team-mate Sheena Sharp, won in the women's 50m prone rifle event, which requires the competitors to fire at a multi-ring target 60 times in just over one hour, from a distance of 50 metres.

'It's about the ability to focus clearly on performing your task again and again and again,' explains Jackson. 'It's very repetitive. In my game, you are trying to hit the middle – 60 times. And in order to hit the middle, you have to get perfect technique and have your head in gear for every single shot.'

HOW THE POWER OF POSITIVE THINKING MAKES A WINNER, BY OSCAR PISTORIOUS

The power of positive thinking is the difference between being at a disadvantage and finding yourself at the top. Just ask Oscar Pistorious. Well, we did on your behalf. Most people would consider having no feet or lower legs a disadvantage, especially in athletics! But Oscar, the South African sprinter, has turned that around to become one of the most famous and successful athletes on the planet.

Using his prosthetic limbs, Oscar, known as 'the Blade Runner', is the World and Paralympic champion in the 200m, and second in South Africa in the able-bodied 400m; all down to a straightforward PMA — Positive Mental Attitude.

'I always say that everybody in their life has some kind of disability or hurdle to overcome,' says Oscar, speaking to *Be a Winner* at the Laureus Sports Awards in St Petersburg. 'But you are not just disabled by your disabilities, you are abled by the millions of other abilities you have. That can overcome any barrier that you have. It comes down to the principle of looking at a negative situation from a different angle and finding the positives.

'If you have a mindset that is negative, you are never going to have a positive outcome. But if you have a positive mindset, even if it's a negative situation, the result is always going to come out more positive, because you will fight for that cause until it comes out more positively. At the end of the day, your influence will eventually turn it around. Give yourself a good kick every now and again!'

To achieve a winning score at the top level, every one of those bullets must come pretty close to bang on target, and that requires intense concentration on a single repetitive act.

'In snooker, your next shot is dependent on where other balls are lying, and in golf, your next shot is dependent on where your last shot landed. Whereas in our sport, it is 60 distinct individual practices that you are performing, and whatever happened in the last shot has no influence on what happens in your current shot, which in turn should have no influence on the next one.'

In other words, Jackson is required to repeat the same action to perfection at a rate of almost once per minute, like a robot. The problem is, she is human, and humans are not perfect, so her task is therefore extremely difficult to perform successfully. So how does she cope with it?

'Everyone is different but I know my own concentration limits, and they're not long! For me, it is about realising the signs of when your concentration is waning and stopping to refocus. It is quite easy to sometimes carry on, and you could be four or five shots in and have dropped a couple before you realise you're not concentrating. You've drifted off.'

Taking time out is, therefore, the key, says Jackson. The brain is an amazing piece of machinery, but if it is overworked, it starts to stutter and splutter. It needs to be rested and reinvigorated. So Susan does just that.

'I take a break, and I completely tune out. Then I come back in, saying, "I've had a mental break, now it's time to focus back in again."'

The other key aspect to top-level performance, as Jackson knows well, is confidence. Not only can a confident individual have faith in his or her own ability, but it strikes fear into others. It also dispels the apparent ill-effects of two of the most overpowering demons – nerves and pressure. Jackson has suffered from both in her career, she says, but she has also learned how to overcome them – through mastery and preparation. If she knows she can do it, and is ready for it, then why should she be worried?

'I think coping with nerves and pressure has a lot to do with self-belief. Why do you get nervous? You get nervous because you doubt your ability. And if you doubt your ability, you have got to look at why you are doubting it. Are you not training? Are you not good enough to be there? Is everyone else better than you? You've got to look at the underlying reason as to why you've got self-doubt. And, therefore, I think you can train people to cope with the pressure by looking beyond the nerves.

'Find me an Olympic champion who doesn't get nervous. Everybody at the top gets nervous, but it comes down to the ability to think "It's OK, I'm prepared." If you are prepared, and you know you are prepared, and what you are doing has just become part of your everyday life, then you would still expect to get nervous in a big situation, but you would be able to say, "I'm ready for this."'

GOLFING SMART

Jackson suggested golf as a sport where outside variables impact on how a player may approach his or her game. Every shot has a direct consequence on the next, both on the green and in the mind. Golf is therefore a game that requires the full range of sporting intelligence, and those that are off the pace can be very quickly singled out. Just keep an eye on the players who are struggling next time you watch a game of golf: pained expressions, slumped shoulders.

Now look at the person at the top of the leader board. Look at how they walk, how they can be at ease and deeply focused at the same time. Golf is the ultimate psychological test, because your toughest opponent is yourself, and mental strength is vital in winning out.

If your ball lands in a bunker on the 18th and you know that if you drop a shot you are out of the game, what do you do then? Your heart is pounding, your legs are shaking and all you can think is, 'If I miss this, I'm out'; how do you deal with that? As you walk up the fairway, with so much time to contemplate the next challenge, the belief that you can pull off the impossible will take you a long way towards actually achieving it.

THERE'S A LOT OF UNTAPPED TALENT OUT THERE, SAYS SCOTLAND'S TOP HOCKEY STAR

Scotland does have a lot of successful junior athletes and teams — but then we let it slip and don't follow through to succeed at senior level. If the talent is there, why don't they make it? The answer, says Scotland hockey captain and GB Olympian Graham Moodie, is down to effort, and it's all in their mind.

'I am coaching at the Glasgow School of Sport just now, and I see some of the kids there and I think, "They are far more talented than I was at that age!" The real stalling point for them is more of a mental thing than a physical thing, because they have all the skills and are obviously talented, but it's whether they want to work harder. Often in sessions when you try to push them harder, some of them can take it and some of them can't.

'I think it's got a lot to do with attitude. Obviously you need the talent but if you don't have the right attitude you won't get anywhere. A lot of people will play for Scotland under-16s and under-18s, but they never make it from there. You could think of any number of reasons why that might be but I think it has a lot to do with how hard you work for it.'

Catriona Matthew is an expert at this. She has been Britain's top-ranked female professional golfer for two consecutive years in 2007 and 2008, and the North Berwick hero knows better than most what it takes to reach the summit and stay there.

'With golf, I would probably say more of it is mental rather than physical. There are players who have done really well without being in good physical shape. I think these days everyone is working on that aspect [of their game] to get more of an edge.'

Matthew was quizzed on all the issues that a golfer may face in a day of competition, and this is how she shaped up:

How do you deal mentally with a bad shot?

CM: Golf is one of these games where it's sometimes tough to remain positive. The main thing is how you recover from a bad shot; you have got to try and not let a bad hole get to you. It doesn't matter if you are Annika Sorenstam or Tiger Woods, you are going to hit a bad shot at some point, but it's how you recover from them that is most important. I know that in a big tournament, even one shot thrown away can make a difference at the end of the year. So if I have a bad hole or make a stupid bogey, I try to slow down a bit to get to the next tee, take a few deep breaths.

Is it difficult to think through each individual shot while looking at the bigger picture of your round?

You get aggressive players and defensive players, and I'm more of a defensive player. I would tend to look and see where you shouldn't land the shot: if there is trouble on the left, and the pin is on the left, you should maybe aim a little bit right. I don't want to be thinking I am going to hit a bad shot, but I have to be aware of the consequences if I happen to.

Do you play it one shot at a time on a difficult course?

That's what you do in your practice runs – you think about where you are going to play a ball and what club you want to use. If you are going to play a par-5, you might want to play just three shots to the hole, because the driver might get you into trouble.

You must have a game plan before you go out there. If you are coming down the last nine holes of a tournament, then it might change a little, but otherwise you need to try and stick to your game plan.

How do you keep your concentration between shots?

You need to forget about it a little once you have hit a shot and you're walking down the fairway. You have your caddy to speak to, or another player. Some people speak more than others and everyone is different, so it's about finding something that suits you.

How do you cope with distractions and background noises when you are trying to concentrate on a shot?

If you hear a noise and it does affect you, you need to be able to stop and start again. It's just something you get used to.

Certain players have something upstairs that means they can go out and dominate a game. Can you understand when people talk about what that is?

Yes. Golf is mostly in the head, so the better you play, the more confident you are. I think if you win a few times, that helps you to win even more, because you are more confident. You have got to be confident. When I first started, I noticed that even at amateur level, the Americans always appeared to be more confident than the British players. It might be down to the culture, the way you have been brought up. You don't need to be arrogant, but you have to have a certain amount of confidence. The better you do, the more confidence you gain.

Is consistency a difficult thing?

I think in golf, more than other sports, it's probably the main thing. You will find everyone can hit the ball just as well, so it's a matter of your bad shots not being too bad.

I would play with people in practice rounds and wonder why they didn't do better in the tournaments. When you're in the top 150 in the world, there is not much to pick between them, just the odd little edge; basically, it comes down to how you cope under pressure. I would be the worst person to play a practice round or a bounce game, because I am usually awful. But come tournament time, I tend to play better.

* * *

Of course, it's all very well for an experienced professional golfer to have such a strong mindset. Catriona Matthew frequently admits that a lot of sporting intelligence, such as concentration and dealing with pressure, comes from experience and 'getting used to it'. But the good news is that there is no minimum standard required. Experience, while helpful, isn't necessary. What is more important is a commitment to developing that intelligence.

THINK LIKE A WINNER, WHOEVER YOU ARE

Yehuda Shinar is credited with helping the England rugby team to their 2003 World Cup success and the Scotland Commonwealth Games team to their record medal haul at the 2006 Games in Melbourne. But he isn't a coach, a psychologist or a guru. Nor does he possess technical expertise in rugby, swimming, cycling or any other sport you care to mention. He is very modest about what he does and doesn't give himself any grand titles.

'I am not a motivator at all,' says the man from Tel Aviv, Israel. 'All I do is teach people how to deal with their challenges. I'm a consultant dealing with elite performance in competitive arenas.'

Essentially, Shinar can teach people how to win. He has devised a set of winning principles that can be applied to any person. He did this by undertaking a study of thousands of people. He defines a winner as someone 'who makes the best use of their personal potential, even when under pressure and/or in competitive situations'.

But note that Shinar says 'elite performance', not 'elite people', when describing what he does. There is a difference. We can't all be elite people. Indeed, it is debatable as to whether 'elite people' exist. What does exist, and what is achievable by everyone, is 'elite performance' – because, as Shinar explains, it can be taught. And, unsurprisingly, it is all in the mind.

What may surprise you, however, is that a winner's necessary mental traits probably aren't the ones you expect. Winners, as Shinar defines them, are not born with natural talent or high IQs. It is much simpler than that: a winner is someone who produces the goods when it is demanded of them.

Shinar's 'winning rules' can help anyone become a high-performance individual.

'The *number one* rule for winners,' he states, 'is that they avoid getting themselves stuck in corners. Their decision-making process leads them to the point that, when it is not necessary to be under pressure, then they won't be. If you put a winner under pressure and say "Tell me yes or no", they will answer when it suits them. If there is an obvious corner they don't want to be in, then they won't be there.'

GET FOCUSED AND SWITCH ON TO YOUR GAME

It was a massive culture shock for football ace Julie Fleeting when she moved from the shivering winters at Scottish grounds to the golden sunshine of California. The highest goal-scorer in Scottish international football history was transferred from amateur ladies side Ayr United to professional American outfit San Diego Spirit, where she was paid to play in front of thousands.

'The girls I was playing with in San Diego were the best in the world. It was a fantastic experience, and I was privileged to have been given the opportunity. There were security guards walking you into your changing-rooms and the stadium was filled with about 8,000 people. I was used to my mum and dad and a man with his dog being at my games! Match-day really couldn't have been further away from what I had experienced at Ayr United.

'I was playing in front of live TV cameras, but for me I think as soon as you get your head switched on to playing a game, it doesn't really matter if I was running out to play for Ayr or San Diego, the main aim for me was that I would do as much as I could for my team to win. You switch on to your own game, then there actually isn't a difference as to which strip you are pulling on and who's watching you. For me, I have simply always wanted to win.'

Shinar cites the French footballer Zinedine Zidane as one of the most natural winners, and deliverers, in the history of sport: a World Cup winner, no less.

'When you watch Zinedine Zidane in a one-on-one situation with the ball at his feet, he prefers not to be there. When players try to tackle him, often he just turns and shows his back to them, thus minimising the pressure! He won't put himself under pressure with dribbling unless he has to. It takes him half a second, and then his decision-making process is easier.'

So, while athletes have to learn to cope with pressure, one approach is to minimise it. But doesn't that defeat the point of being a winner and defy the traits of bravery and intent? Not according to Shinar.

'They want to succeed,' he says. 'They are dedicated to the achievement. Anything that can threaten that accomplishment, they will try to avoid.

You may think this is like running away, but these are the clever ones. If you can, avoid it. But if not, go at it 100 per cent! Why make a decision that could impact negatively on the quality of what you are doing?'

The twelve steps to being a winner are collectively grouped by Shinar into one single criterion: T-CUP – Thinking Correctly Under Pressure. This is how they line up.

1. *Avoiding getting trapped in unnecessary corners* – your ability to avoid being caught under pressure unless strictly necessary.

2. *Patience in creating opportunities* – how much time and effort you are willing to invest in preparing the basic conditions needed to succeed.

3. *Seizing opportunities* – how you make the most of your personal skills and experience in order to realise a given opportunity.

4. *Awareness of faulty tactics/methods* – your ability to realise within a reasonable amount of time that a specific tactic is not working.

5. *Sticking to basics* – getting the simple things consistently right.

6. *Decisiveness* – the degree to which your decision-making process and natural performance are free from unnecessary hesitations.

7. *Maintaining momentum* – how you maintain your highest standards throughout your performance – including staying on top once you get there.

8. *Quality of counter-pressure* – how well you use your personal advantages in one-on-one situations, by taking full advantage of your opponent's weaknesses.

9. *Level of self-control* – how well you maintain the principles of Thinking Correctly Under Pressure by controlling your anxiety and stress.

10. *Sticking to proven tactics* – how strongly you adhere to proven, successful methods in critical situations.

11. *Thoroughness* – the degree to which you are strict and orderly in completing your tasks.

12. *Time management* – putting the time you have to maximum effect.

Shinar's principles showcase sporting intelligence at its very best: they are simple, uncomplicated steps that, if followed correctly, can help any person develop a mindset which is akin to the qualities of sporting intelligence.

We've looked at how much of an impact your brain has on every single decision an athlete makes on the sporting field. We've seen how some of Scotland's most celebrated sports stars use sporting intelligence to their advantage. And we've learned that sporting intelligence isn't limited to the elite end of the competitive arena. Your mind is like your body. It needs to be trained, honed and nourished to perform to its maximum ability. Athletic endeavour is great, but without sporting intelligence you will be off the pace from the outset.

EARN YOURSELF SOME MENTAL WEALTH BY NOTING THESE POINTS . . .

- Concentrate: remain focused on the task at hand. With this comes consistency, alertness and retention of detail. But give your brain a break when you can.
- Be ready to win: have confidence. Confidence comes from preparation. Failing to prepare means preparing to fail.
- Actions under pressure: follow the T-CUP rules laid out by Yehuda Shinar and get the most out of your mind.
- Be positive: a winning mentality is the key to success.

THE EXPERTS' OPINION:

A VIRTUAL GUIDE TO WINNING WITH THE SCOTTISH INSTITUTE OF SPORT HIGH-PERFORMANCE STAFF

The Scottish Institute of Sport, based in Stirling, is the high-performance organisation that helps Scotland's best athletes become even better and challenge for medals on the international stage. They have a panel of experts who advise on everything from the most effective types of strength training to what time an athlete should go to bed each night.

Throughout this book, the panel will be revealing some of the secrets to an athlete's success at the very top level.

MALCOLM FAIRWEATHER
HEAD OF SPORTS SCIENCE AND INNOVATION

Malcolm oversees systems of support across the different disciplines of sports science: physiology, psychology, sports performance and nutrition. His versatility in coaching and consulting at an international level, together with his academic expertise, places him amongst the leading exponents of applied sports science and skill acquisition in the world.

'Chris Hoy never stood out in terms of arrogance, but he really stood out in terms of intention. He would be asking all the time what should he be doing and how should he be doing it. When he meets someone who can offer him that next level, something he can click with, an athlete like Chris will take real advantage of it, because he has the intention.

'I had quite a staggering experience of someone making a statement about what they are going to do and then going on and doing it. In the early 1990s, Donovan Bailey moved from Canada down to Louisiana State University, where I was coaching. I asked him, "What are you doing down here?" And he said he was here to train for the next few years. I asked him what his goal was. And he said, "Oh, it's quite simple. I'm going to be the fastest man there has ever been. I'm going to break the world record." Now, when you hear someone say that, and then you see them do it [Donovan ran a world record 9.84 seconds to win 100m gold at the Olympic Games in Atlanta, 1996] it's staggering. It wasn't his ability that staggered me; it was his patience. The patience to look forward and see the process it took to achieve that.'

5

PLAY UP FOR THE TEAM

WHY WE'RE ALL SUPPORTERS OF BRAVEHEART UNITED

EVERYONE HAS A FAVOURITE TEAM. IT'S USUALLY A collection of sporting heroes able to excite passions when they are winning, and they often incur the wrath and venom of the selfsame supporters when they are losing. Scotland has always been strong when it comes to team games.

It's a history that started a long, long time ago. The 'Big Game' in Stirling was eagerly awaited. On the Scottish side were Braveheart United, a fairly disorganised bunch with pockets of skill and guile and with a highly regarded star player, facing King Eddie's Albion from England, a formidable First Division force with some real bruisers and far greater firepower.

Braveheart United's team captain was a bearded fellow called Willie Wallace . . . it's not known if he was a distant relative of a Hearts, Celtic and Scotland player who played in that great Wembley battle against England in 1967. But the Bravehearts' Willie Wallace was capable of turning a match in his team's favour.

Despite the advantage of a home fixture, Braveheart United weren't expected to progress any further in the Longshanks Cup, not a very popular trophy in Scotland during this time. Stirling looked like the end of their run. This was a life-or-death tie. The English scribes predicted that United would be chopped down to size once again. They wanted Wallace transferred to a club in London with towering ambition. But King Eddie's Albion were known for charging at the defence in numbers and lacking finesse with their finishing. So Wallace began to organise the backline, making sure that Albion's two aces, Marmaduke Tweng and Hughie De Cressingham, were put out of the game for good.

In his pre-match training, Wallace came up with a new tactic. He explained it to the defenders, and they agreed to give it a try. It wasn't four-four-two but the Peter Schiltron defence – named after an English goal minder of that time. When Albion attacked at Stirling Bridge, both Hughie and Marmaduke were neutralised, along with many of their team-mates, when the Scots broke out from their spiky defence and counter-attacked as the English knights stumbled on the narrow bridge. It was a famous victory for the Scots, achieved by Wallace's strict adherence to discipline and teamwork. It was about working together – in adverse conditions – for the greater good. It was fighting for the honour, the badge or the Scottish flag – until the last moment of the battle was over.

He set the trend for the legendary Scottish-born team managers to follow many generations later: people such as Matt Busby, Jock Stein, Bill Shankly, Jim Telfer, Ian McGeechan, Sam Torrance and Alex Ferguson.

Then there are the great Scottish teams of more recent times: the roll of honour includes our football clubs such as Celtic, the first British side to win the European Cup in 1967, and Rangers and Aberdeen, both winners of the European Cup-Winners' Cup. You can include the exploits of the recent Scottish national team – and the Homeless World Cup winners, too. There are the outstanding Scottish rugby sides that have won the Calcutta Cup, Triple Crown and Grand Slam, and who have never failed to make the quarter-finals of a World Cup. We've had Scotland players performing heroics with the British Lions teams on tours of New Zealand, Australia and South Africa. We've had club sides such as Hawick, Gala, Watsonians, Melrose, Boroughmuir and Heriot's, all producing exceptional teams worth recalling.

We've had Scotland's curlers: the battling Chuck Hay, winning the world championship in 1967, with his sons David and Mike repeating the feat in the 1980s; we've seen David Murdoch's victory in the European championships in 2007; and who can ever forget Rhona Martin's team winning Olympic gold in 2002 at Salt Lake City?

We've had the 2006 Commonwealth Games swimmers returning from Melbourne with a record haul of medals. We've had teams in minority sports standing on the podium with the Saltires proudly around their shoulders. On the cricket field, we've seen Scotland improve to take part in the 2007 World Cup in the Caribbean, but it's the Fife cricketers from Freuchie Cricket Club who beat a Surrey side to win the National Village Championship at Lord's in 1985, who still remain particular national heroes.

And even in golf – the archetypal individual sport – we've had Colin Montgomerie, the most outstanding Scottish golfer of the modern era, holing a five-foot winning putt in the Ryder Cup of 2004.

HOW A CAPTAIN CAN INSPIRE A WINNING TEAM, BY GAVIN HASTINGS

Gavin Hastings is one of Scotland's greatest sporting leaders. He captained his country with distinction for several years, encapsulated by many great Murrayfield moments. He also led the British Lions on tour to New Zealand in 1993. So he knows a thing or two about leadership.

'I think my greatest quality was just being on the same level as the players. I wouldn't sit on my high horse. I would make sure that I communicated with my players. People respected me because I was able to engage with my players and get the best out of them: those were my qualities.

'You wouldn't go and sit with your mates all the time when you were having lunch or dinner. You would go and speak to other folk. They weren't your best mates but they were your team-mates, so you engaged with them. If you wanted them to do something for you on the field, or you wanted to motivate them, how the hell could you do that if you never spent any time together away from the field of play?

'It's not rocket science. It's just common sense, and I try not to get into situations or back myself into a corner. By doing that you are reducing the complications and the hassle in your life.'

It gave Europe such a sweet victory over the United States at Oaklands Hill in Michigan. Monty was the wild card who persuaded captain Bernhard Langer that he wanted to be part of the great team. The convincing victory was a supreme team effort, because the Europeans faced the best in the world: Tiger Woods, Phil Mickelson, Davis Love and Jim Furyk. Monty, a man often vilified by the American golfing fraternity and struggling with his form, faced David Toms in the singles. It was a fairytale ending for a great Scot and a memorable team performance.

And what about that British women's hockey team of 1992 winning bronze at the Barcelona Olympics? The team was laced with top Scots, including the legendary Alison Ramsay and Susan and Wendy Fraser; they were the epitome of what a winning team should be, said their coach, a former Olympian himself, Scotland's own Dennis Hay.

'The incredible thing about that team is that they would do anything for each other. You reach a point where it doesn't matter if you like someone or get on with them or not; in terms of the team, you do it because the team will benefit. And when you reach that stage, you can do anything. They were experienced people. There were a whole lot of things that didn't even need to be discussed at that stage, they just knew. It meant a whole lot of time was saved, because we didn't need to discuss trivialities. The major thing was trust, which had been built up over a period of time. It developed confidence to do anything, things that individually they wouldn't have believed they could do.'

And, of course, you can't combine the words teamwork and winning without mentioning the iconic sailor Rodney Pattison – the Scotsman who won three Olympic medals in three consecutive Games with three different partners. Now, there's a guy who knew how to create a winning partnership. In 1968, at the Mexico Games, Pattison teamed up with London solicitor Ian MacDonald Smith to win gold in the 'Flying Dutchman' class; the name of their boat, *Supercalifragilisticexpialidocious*, was promptly shortened to *Superdocious* – probably because the full name wouldn't fit on the side of the boat!

Then at the 1972 Games in Munich, Pattison claimed gold again, this time with Christopher Davies. He won his third and final medal, a silver, in 1976 at the Montreal Games, showing his versatility by competing with yet another partner, Justin Brooke Houghton, with whom he had won the World Championships in 1971.

In every sphere of sport, the Braveheart United legacy lives on in Scotland.

CREATING A WINNING TEAM

So how do you play in a team with such a spirit? And how do you build and develop a true team spirit? Being a team player is different from being an individual, but the basics apply from a school's third hockey team through to the national football side. And as we will see, this also includes individual sportspersons training with national and regional teams. Swimmers, shooters, athletes and badminton players love being part of winning teams, too.

What makes a great team? Walter Smith, the Rangers manager and former Scotland national team coach, should know. His burning desire to win has to be translated to the 11 individuals – often monstrously highly paid and endowed with major egos – on the field every week.

'There is no doubt that in team sport you need a degree of togetherness. Teamwork is the most essential aspect of a team sport. I know that is a bland statement, but it is the formation of a team, the coming together of a team, that is the cornerstone for anything that the team is going to achieve.

'Obviously, teamwork is an essential part of football. Teamwork doesn't just apply to "the team" that runs out onto the park as such. Teamwork is the whole picture and involves the players, the manager, the coaches, the assistants and the medical staff. Everybody is involved in the team. Their aim is to make it as successful as it possibly can be. You always have to remember that,' he says.

'Teamwork spreads from the 11 people on the field at that time to the others and we all become involved in its success. I don't talk about egos; I call it personalities and different types of nature. Not every individual in the team is as competitive or as skilful as some of the others. What you try and get is a common cause. I think one of the easiest ways to gain motivation is for them to have a common cause. It can be to win a championship, as it is here at Rangers, or perhaps for other teams at the bottom of the league to avoid relegation.'

Walter Smith says the mechanics of this do not happen overnight. It can take a few years to get the right people involved at the right time. With a team squad of 20 players, there is only room for 11 and it means nine players a week will be disappointed. He says handling this can be complex – especially when people are dedicated and want to be playing, and winning.

'You can appreciate the disappointment of not being chosen for the team.' He tries to manage each individual, ensuring he knows what he must do for the team. And he has worked closely with many bold personalities in his coaching career, including his current assistant at Ibrox, Ally McCoist, the French star David Ginola and, on two occasions, the former Rangers hero Paul 'Gazza' Gascoigne. Gazza was perhaps one of the most exceptional talents to play in Scotland in the last 20 years, but it was his touch of brilliance which ended Scotland's dreams in Euro 1996 in England that he will probably be best remembered for.

'Gascoigne wasn't actually a difficult player to work with or handle. He enjoyed his football and he likes winning. There wasn't a great deal that you had to do, except for making sure there was the correct environment and a decent balance within the team that allowed him to show his best. And if that was the case, then it was a big plus for the team to have someone of his ability,' says Walter Smith.

And when teams are playing well and performing to their best ability, it is then down to the manager to ensure that they continue to perform, and continue to win.

It is no good to Walter if you win once and then put your feet up: 'You have to keep challenging your players all the time in terms of where they want to be and what they want to achieve.'

Walter Smith likes winners. 'I have an admiration for people who win and not only win once but continue to win. I think that shows a tremendous drive and determination from within the person. Take

Colin Montgomerie, who wins the Order of Merit seven times in a row, or Stephen Hendry, who wins the World Championship seven times in a row. It is a fantastic achievement to keep going and keep winning. That takes far more than just ability.'

TEAMWORK FOR THE INDIVIDUAL

Sir Jackie Stewart – whose biography is entitled *Winning is Not Enough* – would agree with Walter Smith. The tartan-helmeted racing legend might have been the Formula One world champion racing driver three times, but he acknowledges it was his team in the pits that made his success possible. But Sir Jackie also has a reputation for getting things done.

'People know "Jackie will get it done". And there is that confidence starting off,' he says. 'But, to deliver, I need to have a team of people. I won 27 Grands Prix, but I was only part of the team that won. And the reason was, the car didn't break down. To finish first, first you must finish. There's no point in winning the fastest lap or the pole position. I only won about 19 pole positions in my life, but I won 27 Grands Prix because I spent most of the time setting the car up to win, not just to do it for one lap. You need good people to do that. So there is a dependency on the infrastructure.'

US basketball professional Maurice 'Squeaky' Hampton came to Scotland to play with the Scottish Rocks, the pro side based at Braehead Arena. He wanted to help build a successful, winning team, and he knows it cannot be made up only of star players.

In the United States, basketball is a mega-bucks business, one of the top three sports along with baseball and American football; it is followed by tens of millions, so charismatic individuals can earn millions of dollars a year.

Yet teams of prima donna basketball players have consistently failed to blend, as they play as five individuals on the court, rather than one team. But as there are only five players in each team on the court at any one time, it's a fast and very tight space, and there's just no room for inflated egos, says Maurice Hampton.

He says the USA's NBA All Stars team were simply picking big names for the box office – and hoping for success. Yet the All Stars were humiliated by Argentina in the semi-finals at the 2004 Olympics. It was their worst performance in Olympic history. Argentina took the gold, beating Italy in the final.

The angry backlash in America at the All Stars' under-achievement was a wake-up call and the team hammered Lithuania to take a bronze medal. But the selectors had to wake up, too. They decided, in future, to pick a team that would play together, because they realised teamwork was fundamental.

'If you asked me how do you separate team play and individual play, I feel that it all comes down to roles. Everyone defines their role, they know what that is – and they know everyone else's role, too,' says Hampton. 'And once they buy into that, their individual performance contributes to good teamwork. So you identify your role and hold up your end of it, and that's what makes a strong team.'

MAKE SURE THAT THE WHOLE TEAM SHARE IN THE GLORY, SAYS GOAL-SCORING ACE JULIE FLEETING

Julie Fleeting is Scotland's most prolific footballer — with a goal-scoring ratio of almost a goal per game for Scotland — which stood at 100 goals in 101 games. That's more goals than Denis Law, Kenny Dalglish and James McFadden put together!

But, says Arsenal star and European Cup winner Julie, the goals are only the end product of what is a team effort. She doesn't accept the glory and accolades that come with being the one who tucks them away. The real heroes are her team-mates.

'I play alongside very good team-mates. There's no way I could have scored that amount of goals if the players around about me hadn't been of the high standard that they have over all these years.

'The secret is you won't score goals in a team with nobody else playing, and I have been very lucky with the amount of players who have created so many chances for me. I think in Scotland we rely so much on team spirit, working together is something that has always been instilled in Scottish teams. We don't have individuals, we have team players and I would never stay one step ahead if it wasn't for the team. We work well together and scoring is my job. If I'm not scoring I'm not doing my job.'

For Kenny Logan – the former Wasps and Scotland rugby star, who was capped 70 times for his country – the team is *everything*.

'Firstly there is no "I" in team. There's always going to be a star, but the star needs you and you need the star. From a team point of view, especially for me, as a winger, there are a lot of things that need to happen for me to get the ball. You need the other players to do their job right and get into the right positions. And I think a lot of players, wingers especially, need to get in the right position.

'You go out to win the game, that's the most important thing. It doesn't matter who scores the tries. There are games when I have scored tries, but I did nothing, it was everyone inside who made it. I remember Eric Peters scored a try for Scotland against Wales. I ran from my own 22. It was Gavin Hastings, Doddie Weir and then me, and I beat about five or six people. Then I had one man to beat to score the try. I probably could have taken him on, but I just wanted to take him out of the game and pass the ball to Eric, who scored.

'And I'll never forget that when I got up, everybody ran to me, and Eric ran to me after he touched the ball down. He scored, but he knew I had made it. I'll never forget that, because that's what team spirit is all about.'

The title of Alan Sillitoe's book *The Loneliness of the Long-Distance Runner* is often used to talk about the long miles of solitary training for the track athlete. But many top runners, who want to be winners in their own right, like to be part of a team. Better still if it is a Scottish national squad, or even Team GB at the Olympics in Beijing.

Lee McConnell, one of Scotland's leading track stars, said the comfort of team-mates had helped her achieve so much more with her sport.

What gave her the motivation and drive to keep going?

'I just really enjoyed the sport and I had such a good support team around me. I have had quite a few coaches and I have always had a great relationship with them, as well as having a great training squad. That takes away some of the discomfort you have, because at the same time it makes it fun and a hell of a lot easier than being out there on your own. I hate training on my own. I really do not like it, but

EVEN A LITTLE TEAM THAT BELIEVES IN ITSELF CAN HAVE ITS DAY – ARTHURLIE'S FINEST HOUR

Over a century ago, in 1896, Barrhead's local football team, Arthurlie FC, were given a first-round Scottish Cup draw against the mighty Celtic. Even in the days of pigskin balls, ankle-length shorts and handlebar moustaches, Celtic were a massive club and Scottish champions of the 1895–96 season.

By contrast, to this day the occasion is regarded as the only significant on-field event associated with minnows Arthurlie. In his 1942 book, *The Annals of Barrhead*, Robert Murray said of the tie: 'Celtic was then, as now, one of the giants of the game and Arthurlie was, at that time, not regarded as likely to do more than just stave off a farcical defeat.'

I have always had a really good network of people around me; a lot of my friends are athletes and even now the training squad I have is fantastic,' she said.

'We've a pretty good network of friendship outwith the sport as well, and that helps. At training, we're supportive of each other – we pick each other up off the track when we are exhausted, and we support each other to get round and finish the session – which plays a huge part.'

Scott Huggins, 6 ft, 12.5 stone, is a pole-vaulter and although he was born in England, his parents *both* represented Scotland, and he wanted to carry on the family tradition.

'I love the way that the Scots are really patriotic about their sport and about their country, whereas down in England they sometimes don't really seem to care. When I am representing Scotland, I like the atmosphere in the teams. I am greeted into the team regardless of my accent [Scott has a strong London accent]. You don't feel that in the English teams, really. Obviously, you get on with people, but it's always about the individual rather than the team. It feels like a real "Scottish Team".

'I was going for a Scottish National record and the Scottish team came down to England, and they were on the other side of the track in the stands, all clapping. It was the loudest clap I have ever heard, and they were on the other side of the track. That was a big highlight for me,' he recounts.

Rather than be overawed by the occasion, Arthurlie instead took a pragmatic approach to the game. Their inspiration was obvious and their motivation was easy: to do well against stronger opposition. It was their one chance in life to go down as never-to-be-forgotten in Scottish football records, and they wanted to make sure they weren't passed over as a small bump on the road of Celtic's stampede to another trophy.

And while Arthurlie's players were preparing for the biggest match of their lives, Celtic's Victorian prima donnas were in the middle of an internal quarrel with the club. Several of their players were on strike, either due to dissatisfaction at the wage they received or because they were sulking at recent criticism in the press. They actually started the game a couple of men short. On the day, Arthurlie were, quite simply, more inspired. With their home support behind them, they won the game not by a hair's breadth, but resoundingly, thumping the then First Division leaders 4–2.

This sounds very similar to what Scotland's swimmers have to say. Gregor Tait, one of Scotland's finest swimmers and the Commonwealth Games 200m backstroke and a 200m medley gold medallist, loves the team environment when he is training with his Scottish colleagues.

'One thing that keeps me coming back to the sport is our team. There are 13 or 14 of us at the moment, and it is a team atmosphere. You pull each other along: we are 99 per cent team and 1 per cent individual. We look after each other. If someone isn't having a good day, we pull them up; if someone's having a great day, we try to latch on to it. It's just like any other team. People don't realise that swimming can be a team sport, but right until that moment when you stand at the block, I know my team-mates are behind me, and everyone is wanting me to do well,' he says.

And even badminton players, such as Imogen Bankier and Emma Mason, Scotland's top double act and one of the most successful duos in Britain, see themselves as a team of two. Their very different characters complement each other. Imogen embodies intensity and focus while Emma is more casual and ready to chill out after a tough session, but their differences gel on court.

'I've got a good serve and I'm strong at the net, whereas Emma's a really good mover and powerful from the back,' says Imogen. 'I think we work well together in that way, but we've also practised a lot the other way around. Emma's worked on her serve and net play, and I've worked on my rear courts. It's about working together, that's the main thing.'

Bankier believes that a successful partnership is based on a respectful, reciprocal working rapport. She has recently reached a world ranking of 12 with her new mixed-doubles partner, Robert Blair.

'I'm really good friends with my partners, and that helps, because if you don't get on, then you can't gel or have good chemistry on court. You've got to be communicating all the time, whether it's about what you're going to do, what you're thinking or what's going to happen.'

Respect is an essential part of being a successful team, something you must have for those around you, even if you feel that they are not as accomplished or talented as you. It is your job to help and improve the rest of the team by giving encouragement and support.

AN ALL BLACK LEGEND GIVES HIS WINNING INSIGHT

If you want to know what it takes to lead a successful team, it is difficult to find a man who has done so with more success than All Black legend Sean Fitzpatrick. Sean won the World Cup with New Zealand in 1987, and went on to be one of his country's most successful captains.

What are the key factors to building a successful team?

SF: I think the culture of the organisation is something we talk about a lot – sustaining a culture of success. And we talk about the success we've had and the failures we've had, and then building up a team that is just totally focused on winning, playing the best players week in, week out. And honouring the jersey with what it deserves. Our goal hasn't changed in the last 120 years – to be the best team in the world and win every game we play.

How does a winning team keep winning?

Well, you enjoy your success, and then you park it. We talk a lot about our failures and why we failed. I think some of the teams that have failed did so because they enjoyed their success for too long. For me, when people ask me what the most 'memorable' game I had for the All Blacks was, I say, without question, that it was in 1993, when we lost to the British Lions. That was the worst game I had for them, and I think about it a lot, because I never want to go back there. The luxury of being involved in a team environment is that you are forever challenging each other to do better, and to do everything you can to win. And if you see another team member slacking, you jump all over them like a rash, and make sure they change their attitude.

When your team is down and out, what do you do to make sure you come back stronger?

Well you've got to re-evaluate. We lost the World Cup in 1991, and we just had to go away and re-evaluate who we were. We had to be brutally honest and say, 'Actually, we're not the best team in the world, I'm not the best hooker in the world, and I've got to start again. I've got to be fitter, I've got to be faster, I've got to be stronger. I've got to respect the jersey because I lost my respect for it.' All those things: it's about being honest. I'm not a huge fan of having mission statements written on the walls, but at the end of the day we say at the All Blacks that it's a 24/7 job; once an All Black, always an All Black. The values you have at home in terms of respect and honesty, you have them at work, too.

How do you lead a winning team?

Leadership is such a basic thing. If you are honest and you respect people, people will respect you. They don't necessarily need to like you, but as long as they respect you, you're halfway there.

What is so good about being in a team?

My father was also an All Black. I was kicking the ball around the back yard with my brother, and Dad stopped mowing the lawn and came over and said, 'Look boys, there are two things. The first is that you don't have to play rugby. All I want is that you play a team sport, and that you enjoy it.' You gain so much from being on a team.

And then, making sure you enjoy it is pretty crucial. Another thing is treating everyone as an equal.

And finally, all we are trying to do is to be as successful as we can be. If you think about that, not everyone is going to be an All Black, not everyone is going to play for Scotland, not everyone will be an Olympian. But we can each achieve the highest we can achieve personally by being as successful as we can. We can sleep easy at night and retire happily.

YOU CAN'T DO IT ON YOUR OWN – COMMUNICATION IS KEY, SAYS OLYMPIC HERO SHIRLEY ROBERTSON

Double Olympic sailing champion Shirley Robertson has experienced her sport from a solo and a team perspective. In 2000 she won individual gold in the Europe Class at the Sydney Games, then in Athens in 2004 she led her three-woman crew to Yngling Class gold with one race to spare. But both medals were a team effort, Shirley told *Be a Winner.*

'In Sydney, I felt a bit of a fraud standing there on my own with a gold medal, because it had actually been such a team effort. So many people gave up so much. I never would have won without the coach that I had. We had such good respect for each other and such determination to make it happen.

'Then in Athens, I had a guy called Ian Walker, who had been a team-mate in Sydney. He joined us and we had no money, crew missing and we didn't have a boat, but between us we made it happen. He was certainly the fourth member of the team. You can't do it on your own, you need help. Especially now that even the smallest countries are so professional in every sport that you've got to take all the help you can get.

'Our team was really good at not "stamp collecting". You know, when you are married, and your partner keeps leaving their socks on the floor, and you don't say anything? Then eventually it all explodes, and you have a massive argument? Well, we were all very keen not to do that within the team, so we always debriefed the day and tried to keep the communication going. It was always part of the routine. We discussed what we were going to do for the day, and often in the boat there would be heated discussions, but we would always talk about it.'

SO WHAT IS SCOTLAND'S GREATEST TEAM?

But perhaps one of Scotland's greatest team coaches was Jock Stein, who was manager of Celtic Football Club when they won the European Cup in 1967 and later became the Scotland team manager. According to Billy McNeil, captain of the Lisbon Lions, Jock Stein 'would always tell you to play for your strengths and disguise your weaknesses. He insisted you helped out a colleague who might not have been having the best of days. He told you, in the next game, it might be your turn to need assistance. He kept it simple. Big Jock never asked anyone to do something he didn't believe they had the skills to cope with. We had a real mixture of players at Celtic Park, and he was the man who fused all this talent together.'

Team-building is a special talent; but being part of a team is also something special. And if that team is winning, successful and has an indomitable team spirit, then this is as good as it gets being a Scottish sportsperson. This is the Braveheart United legacy – and you are part of that proud history.

THE FACTS THAT MATTER FOR ALL WINNING TEAMS . . .

- Stick together: the crux of any successful team is that they support each other, no matter what.
- Create a common goal: a group of individuals does not make a team. If you are all striving in the same direction, you have more chance of success.
- Challenge and help each other: the benefit of a team is that there is always someone to assist you or push you forward, and you in turn can help them.
- Respect each other: everyone has strengths and weaknesses. Use this to your advantage, build on your strengths and address your weaknesses.

THE EXPERTS' OPINION:

KEITH JOSS
WOMEN'S HIGH-PERFORMANCE/NATIONAL TEAM HOCKEY COACH

Keith manages the women's hockey programme as well as the day-to-day coaching responsibilities of the national team, working with and responsible for up to 30 players in the squad.

'The learning curve is essential. At some point, you have to endure that learning curve. Our male players endured that learning curve when they were 15, when they went to play Holland. The Dutch are on a pedestal. They have a perfect regime, massive player pools and more artificial pitches in one of their towns than we have in the whole of Scotland. We said, "We will go out with a plan, have a go at the Dutch." We got beat 4 or 5–1, but by the time they were under-18s, three years later, they beat Holland 5–2. Those guys are now going into games knowing they are just playing against other human beings.'

6

THE AUSSIE RULES – AN EXAMPLE FOR SCOTLAND?

WE'VE HEARD LOTS OF GREAT SUCCESS STORIES ABOUT Scottish sport in the last five chapters. But now it's time for a few home truths. Scotland has produced some amazing athletes and wonderful winners in its history. But for every winner, or team of winners, there are countless others who have failed to realise and fulfil their potential.

But it isn't a problem that arises through lack of ability in Scotland. We have plenty of talent, tonnes of potential. It is a problem we face through lack of ambition and killer instinct. Sport, when it comes down to it, is clinical. It is merciless. If you don't want it enough, someone else will take it.

THE SCOTS: 'AIM LOW AND AVOID DISAPPOINTMENT'

In Scottish culture today, there is, in some quarters, a negative attitude when it comes to achievement and aspiration: we don't like people getting above their station, because if we fail, we will be scorned, laughed at and humiliated.

'DON'T TALK ABOUT IT – DO IT!' THAT'S THE AUSSIE WAY OF WINNING

Australians love thrashing anyone at sport. Michael McCann and his hockey contemporaries are no exception. McCann is the star-scorer of 72 goals in six years for the Australian national side, the Kookaburras, and his team has created a true dynasty of achievement since the turn of the century. As well as winning Olympic gold in Athens 2004, McCann, from Sydney, has in his collection two Commonwealth gold medals, a World Cup silver medal and two Champions Trophy silver medals.

A winning mentality, according to the Australian, all comes back to having the right attitude and work ethic. From there, the mentality will come as part of natural progression.

'It has to be bred in you,' explains McCann. 'There are a lot of people who will talk about working very hard, but in Australia you don't talk about it, you do it. People see you doing it and they follow you to do it.

'A lot of our senior players breed it into you. At 35 they are still doing all the work. They are still doing the work because they have to set an example for the younger guys. That's what I try to do when I am back in New South Wales, I do the running with the younger guys. I have to push myself harder so these guys have to catch me and try to win the time trials. Not because I'm fitter, but because I don't want to let them feel like they can ease up because they beat a player who was in the national team.'

Sad but true, that's how too many people think in Scotland. When we do see glimpses of glory, more often than not it ends in bitter disappointment, so not bothering in the first place is the way many people deal with it. It is an attitude that was identified in 2006 in a research study carried out by the University of Stirling for the Winning Scotland Foundation, investigating relationships between sporting success and aspects of Scottish culture.

The study, called *Culture of Winning in Scottish Sport*, explained how the national press states that 'our sportsmen and women can't win' and that Scotland is 'a nation starved of sporting success'. It also commented that 'we often have frequently over-enthusiastic expectations of continued success'.

A number of reasons for this collective social outlook are highlighted, one being an over-nostalgic recollection of past achievements – Archie Gemmill's goal against Holland in the 1978 World Cup is frequently recalled as an inspirational moment in Scottish sport, while the embarrassment of the actual campaign is often forgotten.

Another is our culture and national pride being linked to sporting achievement. Take the Tartan Army, the national football team's much-loved fan club, for example: clad in kilts, navy football shirts with the Scottish badge proudly emblazoned, and in some cases the famous 'See you Jimmy' caps, they proclaim their patriotism through their support of the team.

The study also emphasises the Scottish 'tendency to criticise and focus on what is wrong with something, rather than to praise, appreciate and be positive'. When the national football team drew France and Italy in the Euro 2008 qualifiers, certain newspaper headlines read: 'Heaven Alp Us', 'Vogts' Nightmare Followed by Impossible Dream' and 'Scots rue the draw from hell'. It gives the impression we had given up before we even got started. Optimism and positivity were turfed out in exchange for drama and despair: if we aim low, we will avoid disappointment. Fortunately Walter Smith and then Alex McLeish did not share this attitude.

All in all, the general implication is that, as a society, Scots don't aspire to win enough, and that when they do, they usually 'bottle it', 'choke' or fail to live up to the pressures of expectation. It is a culture of expecting to lose.

THE AUSSIES: 'AIMING EVER HIGHER'

The good news is that a culture of winning is achievable in Scotland. It is not impossible to turn the mood of a nation around. And that isn't a lofty statement with no substance, because it has been achieved in other countries around the world, Australia being the most well-known example.

In 1976, Australia had a dismal Olympic Games in Montreal, failing to win anything, and bringing home just one silver and three bronze medals. It was deemed a national catastrophe in Australia, a country that, like Scotland, prided itself on sporting achievement. In 1981, to address the issue, Prime Minister Malcolm Fraser created the Australian Institute of Sport (AIS), an organisation dedicated to providing coaching for elite athletes in a number of sports, in order to prepare athletes to compete and win on the world stage.

The AIS has proved to be an exceptional success in developing winners. In the three Olympic Games before Beijing 2008 – Atlanta 1996, Sydney 2000 and Athens 2004 – the Australians averaged more than 30 medals (including seven golds); Australia has turned its fortunes around to become, per capita, the most successful sporting nation on the planet.

The USA and China may claim to win more medals, but, using the Athens Olympics as a measure, for every one Olympic medallist the USA produces, Australia will have 15 and for every one China produces, Australia will have 65.

WHY HARD-HITTING AUSSIES ARE A SPORTING INSPIRATION

The Australians are to cricket what Brazilians are to football, what New Zealanders are to rugby. Unparalleled, for the most part, Australia are unbeatable. One of their greatest exponents was captain and batsman fantastic Steve Waugh. His view on why the Aussies were so dominant is quite simple, and easy to emulate for budding world-beaters everywhere.

'I guess it was all about pride in our performance and always trying to lift the bar. We always knew how well we could play and couldn't accept playing below that standard, so we were always trying to improve and raise the bar. There were always people trying to get your spot on the team,' said Steve, speaking to *Be a Winner* in St Petersburg in 2008.

'It means a lot to play for the side. When you go out there, there is a history and tradition you want to uphold. It's really all about pride in your performance. Being the best side in the world is about being consistent for long periods of time. After the 2005 Ashes, England let themselves down with their planning and preparation, and they haven't recovered since. You can't win one series, then lose the next one 5–0. If that was Australia, the whole team would have been dropped.'

Besides Olympians, the AIS has also produced athletes of such calibre as rugby World Cup-winning captain John Eales, World Cup-winning and world-record-holding cricketer Glenn McGrath (most international wickets by a fast-bowler) and Premiership (and former Celtic) footballer Mark Viduka.

At the front door of the AIS headquarters stands a statue that is there to inspire the hundreds of elite athletes that walk past it every day. It is a bronze cast of a pole-vaulter in mid-flight, clinging to his pole, conquering the heights. But he isn't jumping over anything – there is no bar. This isn't because the sculptor forgot to put one there, it is because 'a bar' represents 'a barrier', and the AIS don't want their athletes to feel that there is a barrier to what they can achieve. The 'no bar' metaphor of the statue relates directly to the mindset of the athletes. There is no limit to what they can achieve.

The impact of this statue is reinforced by the AIS slogan: *The race for excellence has no finish line. In Australia, the race starts at the Australian Institute of Sport.* That is how they operate. No bar, no line, no limits.

SCOTLAND V AUSTRALIA

Scotland, as a nation, isn't unlike Australia. Its people have a similar social personality, jovial, friendly and welcoming. Scots, like the Australians, love their sport, and enjoy a drink (or two, or three). They also share a similar history of sporting achievement and participation, and a desire to beat England at all costs.

On the sports field, Scotland against Australia would deliver some differing results, depending on the discipline. We would like to think we could beat them in football, but it would be a close call (and it would be interesting to see Celtic's Scott McDonald squaring up to his club captain, Stephen McManus). In rugby, it might go the other way, in favour of the Wallabies, but again it is always a tough one to predict. However, we can safely assume that Scotland would probably edge it in cricket . . .

OK, maybe not. The last time the Scots and the Aussies met in cricket was during the group stages of the 2007 Cricket World Cup in the West Indies, when the men from Down Under sprinted to a 203-run victory. To put it simply, they thumped Scotland.

The Scots went into the game confident that they could at least rattle the Australians. After almost leading his men to a scalping of Pakistan in the summer of 2006, Scotland's World Cup captain Craig Wright was pragmatic about his team's chances in their tournament opener.

'We will take the field against Australia with the intention of doing everything we can to win. But, considering we are coming up against the top team in the world, the odds are massively stacked against us. From our point of view, a satisfactory World Cup would be to really show the cricketing world that Scotland are a good team. And if that means putting up a good performance against Australia and losing, we will be disappointed, but if we can compete well, it will be a massive feather in our cap.'

Unfortunately, as we know, Craig's cap remained featherless, but the match itself went some way to defining the difference in sporting norms between the two countries. Never expected to win, the Scots looked as though they might be able to contain the mighty Aussies. However, when the champions sensed an opportunity, they went for the kill, as this BBC report states:

> Scotland's bowlers looked like they might restrict Australia to under 300 runs at one point, but Brad Hogg smashed 40 off 15 balls as he and Shane Watson added 53 runs off the last four overs. In reply, Scotland were soon reeling as the top order failed to cope with Australia's attack, in which veteran Glenn McGrath took three wickets operating as first change . . . as he took 3–14 from six overs.

The Aussies could have relented if they pleased and finished the match in cruise control, but that isn't the way of the Australian cricket team, which has been the best side in the world for the past ten years, winning three consecutive World Cups (1999, 2003 and 2007). They don't hang back after they go ahead, nor do they go easier on a team perceived to be weaker. They go out to win, as hard as they can and as well as they can, every time. That is what winners do.

Now, when have we seen Scotland do that? Or, to put it another way, how many times have you seen Scotland go into a match they were supposed to win by a considerable margin and end up being turned over by relative minnows? In the Euro 2008 qualifiers, after defeating classy France in Paris and then thrashing fancied Ukraine at Hampden, when it came to the bread-and-butter fixture against Georgia, a win for Scotland was almost a certainty, wasn't it?

Well, so you would think. But Alex McLeish's men took their foot off the gas, and went down 2–0, effectively ending their chances of qualification for the tournament. How could they lose to a team like Georgia, after the wins they had just recorded? Yes, Scotland were carrying some injuries, but they should still have beaten a bunch of part-timers without any difficulty, as Australia did to the Scottish cricket team. So why did it happen? And why will we probably never see Scotland beat Australia in cricket?

'The Australians have a different outlook on sport and, to an extent, on life in general,' explains Craig Wright, Scotland's World Cup captain, who has played top-level summer cricket in Australia during the Scottish off-season. 'My experience is in cricket, and it isn't fair to compare Scottish cricket to Australian cricket. But even if you compare UK cricket there is a difference, a different mentality and a different sporting culture. I think perhaps in Scotland we have a more spectator-like approach to sport, rather than actually going out and doing it.

'I think the Australian sporting culture comes from the fact that sport is very much embedded in what they do as a nation. Everyone gets the opportunity to play any number of sports when they are young, then they find one that they want to continue in. And because there are so many people playing sport, to get to the top of that sport you have to be something special. Ability isn't enough, because there's so much competition. You have to have the ability and also the attitude. There may be 20 or 25 players competing for one spot in a team, whereas in this country we may only have, well, one! There are so many people in Australia aspiring to get to the level required to play international sport.'

'EVEN THE KING NEEDED TO LEARN TO HONOUR THE GAME'

Denis Law remains one of Scotland's greatest footballers. He won a European Cup medal with Manchester United in 1968 and was capped 55 times for Scotland, scoring a record of 30 goals that remains today, equalled only by Kenny Dalglish. But he wasn't a born legend. He had to learn some respect. John Rafferty, one of Scotland's finest sportswriters, made this fascinating insight into the young Law in *The Observer*, in November 1958 before he moved to Manchester City, Torino and then Manchester United:

Denis Law, a slim, blond, whiffy-haired youth affecting a colourful modern style of dress, is, at 18 years of age, the youngest player to be capped for Scotland since RS McColl 60 years ago. Such has been his success at Cardiff last month and at Hampden Park last week that on sheer football ability his selection for Scotland's team for years to come would seem to be more or less automatic.

Unfortunately, it is not just as simple as all that. There is a small question of field conduct occupying many of the minds that matter. This, to some, may seem strange, for it was those same minds which conceived the 'rummel 'em up' international tactics which disgraced Scotland just a few years ago. After the Hampden game on Wednesday Law was credited with having played to orders and worried and harried Danny Blanchflower off his game. This, of course, went a long way to disrupting the Irish attacking rhythm. Yet it was generally deplored later that young Law had been too rough about his task.

It does seem all wrong that a youngster of no more than school age should be roughing a world celebrity and football master such as Blanchflower. Later the Irishman complained bitterly that he had never been kicked so much in a game but when asked about Law would say: 'If that is him at 18 I would not like to play against him when he is 24.' But this is not the first occasion on which the young Huddersfield forward has drawn attention to himself. At Cardiff, in his first international, he had to be reprimanded by the referee for showing signs of retaliation when the game became hot — and him only 18, too. Then it is a fact that every time the selectors watched him before he was chosen, he was spoken to by the referee for serious breach of rules.

The selectors may have found an inside forward but, at the same time, they have bought themselves a bit of trouble. It was inevitable this should happen, for Law has been described as resembling rock 'n' roll singer Tommy Steele in appearance and former international forward Billy Steel in his play. It is just too much to resemble two such turbulent characters.

Law, at a very moderate 18 years of age, is a long jump from the small, slim, 15-year-old boy sent from Aberdeen to Huddersfield to begin his football apprenticeship. He had been spotted by the brother of manager Andy Beattie, playing for Powis School. When he arrived at Huddersfield station, the waiting officials did not recognise him. No wonder. He looked so frail and slight, and he wore thick glasses to correct a squint. This has gone and so have the spectacles. Now, after working on the ground staff and graduating through Huddersfield's five teams, he stands a slim, wiry and confident athlete. He favours the clothes liked by those youths who bounce to the modern dance rhythms — the narrow trousers, the colourful socks, the elaborate footwear. He has all the brashness and love of a good time of that group.

Of his football ability there is no doubt. His fitness to be a profitable member of Scotland's team for the next ten years at least is equally clear. There is just this business of having him conform to the conventions. That is not so easy either. Try to change his style, try to tone him down too much, and as sure as a gun he will be ruined as a footballer. His cheek and lack of respect for the opposition go a long way to making him the player he is. Goodness knows, we have had too many players showing too much respect for so long. We may say we do not like cheeky boys, but we must admit that when it comes to winning, a bit of cheek goes a long way and that goes for football, boxing, running or any other sport.

Perhaps the modern, luxurious international atmosphere with the five-star elegance of Turnberry and the understanding of Matt Busby [then the Manchester United and Scotland national team manager] will take the rough edges off young Law. But for goodness' sake don't let us go too far and stifle him. Just ensuring that cheek does not become a big-head would be enough.

IMPLEMENTING A CHANGE

So, in Scotland we must try to think differently. We must aim higher. We must see that by staying within the safety net of where we feel comfortable, and thinking we will avoid losing by not aspiring to win, we are placing predetermined limits on what we can achieve. By keeping the bar set low, it is difficult to reach the heights, let alone remove limits altogether.

Measures have already been taken to improve Scottish sport at an elite level. Since it was conceived in 1998, and prior to the Beijing Olympics, the Scottish Institute of Sport has supported athletes who have achieved an impressive 12 World Championships; two Olympic gold medals, four Olympic silver medals; 11 gold, nine silver and six bronze Paralympic medals; 12 gold, 11 silver and 18 bronze Commonwealth Games medals; six European Championships; and one gold and two silver medals at the European Youth Olympics. Its supported athletes include one Wimbledon champion; one US Junior Open tennis champion; one European golf tour professional; six rugby players with international caps and one British Lion; and 16 hockey players capped for Great Britain.

The Institute's greatest success has been the establishment of a high-performance system inspired by the vision of Scotland consistently winning on the world stage. They even brought in an Aussie to make sure the job was done correctly: for almost three years, from September 2004 to summer 2007, Marty Aitken was the Scottish Institute of Sport's Director of Performance (he then returned to his hometown, Melbourne, to work with the Victorian Institute of Sport). A top rower, cyclist and skier in his own athletic career, it was as a world-class coach that he really displayed his winning credentials. In a 16-year professional coaching career, he was head coach to the British and Swiss national rowing teams, and he has overseen eight gold, seven silver and six bronze medals at either World Championship or Olympic level.

So where does Marty, who is as close as you can get to having informed expertise on the sporting mindset of both countries, feel the changes need to be made for Scotland to embrace Australia's winning culture?

GETTING THERE IS JUST THE BEGINNING

Being selected to represent a team, be it your school, your local club or even your country, is a great achievement. But just because your name is on the list doesn't mean you have made it. In elite sport, athletes are judged on their performance in the arena. Simply being there counts for nothing unless they can deliver the goods.

By his own admission, 30-year-old slalom-canoeist Campbell Walsh was far from impressed by his performance in the final GB selection race for the 2008 Olympics. Although he was a silver medallist in Athens four years earlier, and a hot tip to do the same again, or better, in Beijing, Walsh was disappointed because he let his own high standards slip, finishing 16 seconds behind the winner.

'I train to perform well and today wasn't a performance. I even missed a gate and had to paddle back for it,' said the Glaswegian. 'To be honest, I'm more annoyed about my race than thinking about the fact I've qualified for the Olympics.'

So even though his ticket to China had been booked, he knew there was only one way that he would be bringing a medal back with him.

'I'll win an Olympic gold if I perform to the best of my ability,' he said.

'In Australia, it is accepted that sport is a part of growing up. So the parents expect the kids to do sport. We have a big supporting crowd, and they will watch any sport. And if you have that, people strive to be in the spotlight. The kudos comes from actually being a successful sportsman in Australia, which is not the case here. If you play football or rugby, you get a crowd to those things, but in Australia you get a crowd to anything! This is something that is hard to change in Scotland. It needs to change at Phys Ed level in schools, and then maybe within the family. It's a long process.'

As Marty points out, the spectator in Australia is a more varied sports fan. He or she will watch anything. Not only is this encouragement for young athletes to strive for the limelight, but also it means all sports are 'socially acceptable' and 'cool' to play. You are an athlete first, for which you should be praised; your actual discipline is irrelevant. There is a common conception here in Scotland, not helped by the media and the public fan-base, that unless you play professional football, rugby, golf or tennis, you may as well not bother, because nobody cares. Aitken believes that the differences between how the public gauge national sport and athletes in Australia and in Scotland are significant.

'Kids need to aspire to be like the winners, and so winners at the top level in Scotland are important as role models. This needs to happen in football and rugby first, then try to get as much exposure in the press as possible for the other sports that are winning. It's the only way.'

In Australia, the media are a lot more supportive of good results. They are critical of bad results, but they don't go on and on about it, because it is self-perpetuating: 'If you slate people enough, they are going to believe they are rubbish.'

But to change the culture and adopt the 'Aussie Rules' requires us, as participants, fans, spectators and consumers of sport, to take action. Where do we begin?

Well, starting from the bottom up is usually a good idea. For most Scots, sporting careers start at school. Similarly, our attitudes towards sport are also moulded in our developmental years in the classroom. However, this system suffered a mortal blow in the 1980s, when a nationwide strike resulted in teachers who once took after-school sports classes voluntarily, suddenly demanding payment. The result was a generation of youngsters, now in their thirties and forties, deprived of sport at school. There was a 90 per cent drop in kids playing football at school during this period, and a fall of 75 per cent in schoolboy rugby.

Thankfully, things are on the up again, but even today, there are problems with the way school sport is organised. Take rugby, for example. Aside from an annual tournament – the Bell Lawrie Scottish Schools Cup – there is no competitive rugby for young players. The vast majority of schoolboy players will only enjoy, at most, half a dozen meaningful matches per season. Scotland Rugby's head coach, Frank Hadden, himself a former schoolmaster and coach at Merchiston Castle in Edinburgh, explains the merits a more competitive structure could bring:

'For me, the most frustrating thing about Scottish rugby is the lack of competition and intensity at junior level. It means that almost all the serious development has to be done after the player leaves school, whereas, in Australia, school games are in front of thousands of people, and you are doing 12 training sessions a week. I taught in Australia for a while, and their school league system has been going since the 1800s. We haven't even got a league yet. And you cannot create the intensity required to develop players unless you have the sort of competition that inspires people and makes it really worth winning. At the boarding schools, the whole school would watch on the touchline, and as you went through the school, you really wanted to be in the First Fifteen.

'You need that motivation. You can't just play for the sake of playing, you need something that inspires you, and it is extremely frustrating to me that we don't have that in Scotland. The cup competition is fine, but what happens if you go out after two games?' asks Hadden, who led Scotland to the Calcutta Cup in 2006 and 2008.

A further disincentive is the lack of attention that many sports receive, which, of course, reduces their chances of becoming more popular with the general public. Scottish cyclist Chris Hoy worries that not only is there a lack of positivity surrounding Scottish sport, but that it is too often dominated by one or two sports, leaving the rest – including his – to feed off scraps of column inches and air-time. The problem is that this then defines the nation's attitude towards sport. If the football team or the rugby team loses, then Scotland despairs, often without knowing what hundreds of other Scottish athletes are achieving in dozens of other sports all over the world.

'I think it would be good for other sports to get some of the attention that football seems to dominate,' says Hoy. 'I think the sports should get the attention they deserve in terms of success. Unfortunately in athletics, which is very high profile and receives a lot of attention, British athletes aren't doing that well, compared to ten or twenty years ago.

'It would be nice if the British public, like the Australians, celebrated their winners. If there is a successful team or individual in any sport, they will watch them on telly and celebrate their success. It doesn't seem to be that way in Britain. It may sound like sour grapes, the minority sportsman saying that, but it is frustrating. It's not that we want attention or more money, we just want some balance and fairness.'

Catriona Morrison, world champion duathlete, agrees with Hoy that we should take a more Antipodean approach to sport in Scotland:

'I think a lot of other countries value their athletes a lot more as part of their culture. In Australia or New Zealand, you could turn round to the back of a cereal packet and see a triathlete, and that guy is a hero, whereas in this country you turn round to the back of a cereal packet and it probably says "add three spoonfuls of sugar"!

'Scotland doesn't champion success at all. We don't necessarily accept losing, but we certainly expect to lose. We would rather have a hard luck story over someone saying "I've done very well and I'm at the top of my game", because it is not a story. What makes stories is that they are heart-rending, they are human and they are scandalous. "Pat on the back" stories don't really sell papers, to be honest.'

The Edinburgh swimmer Gregor Tait, live on BBC TV, won two gold medals for Scotland at the Commonwealth Games in 2006. He did receive quite a few column inches – and even an appearance on Andrew Marr's weekend TV show, *Sunday A.M.* – but the hype surrounding him and several of his equally successful team-mates didn't last long.

'Swimming's not as high profile as it should be. In Scotland, cycling and swimming have been the two most successful sports for the last six years or so, but you could probably go and ask a guy outside to name a swimmer and he wouldn't have a clue. He might say Ian Thorpe. Football and rugby are the high profile ones, that isn't going to change. Don't get me wrong, I love football and I'm starting to get into rugby more, but I just think that the best Scottish swimmers should be well known, they should be able to walk down the street and someone go "I recognise that guy – that's one of those swimmers."'

SOME INSPIRATION – THOSE WHO DARE TO BE

Scotland has a whole host of athletes who are the best in the world at what they do, yet they receive little or no praise in the public arena. Among others, we have Nicole Arthur, a teenage world champion waterskier from Slamannan, near Falkirk; Ruaridh Cunningham, the world junior downhill mountain bike champion from Melrose in the Borders; Lawrence Tynes from Greenock, an American Football goal-kicker who won the Super Bowl in 2008 with the New York Giants; and Edinburgh tennis star Graeme Dyce, the junior Australian Open doubles champion in 2007.

CATHY FREEMAN – HERO OF SYDNEY 2000

Who can forget Cathy Freeman's performance of a lifetime over 400m on 'Magic Monday' at the 2000 Sydney Olympics? In front of over 70,000 expectant fans, she delivered the performance of her life, fulfilling the expectations of millions of Australians all over the world, and especially ethnic Aborigines in her homeland. Between 1994 and 2004 she won 25 of the 30 major championship races in which she competed. So what lies behind her phenomenal success?

As in most sports, track and field athletics has professionalised physical training and conditioning to new and sophisticated levels over the last two decades, and any athlete who aspires to World or Olympic glory has to follow training and conditioning routines that are well known to coaches and scientists throughout the world.

It follows, therefore, that the bodies of all elite athletes are honed to a state of near-perfection, so what separates the winners from the losers? For Freeman, the difference between winning and losing was more to do with heart, mind and spirit than with the near-perfect conditioning of her body for the 400m event. Freeman explained the difference for her lay within her:

- Heart — her passion to win, which came from a love of running and winning; running was like flying, without restriction.

- Mind — an inner strength and mental belief that she would win every race she entered, safe in the knowledge that her training and preparation were so detailed in nature that nothing was left to chance.

- Spirit — being at one with the various communities in her life — her family, friends, neighbourhoods, Australia and the whole Aborigine nation. Her purpose was greater than individual, personal success.

An athlete without a healthy and positive mental attitude is about as efficient as a Formula 1 racing car with flat tyres.
                                                              — Cathy Freeman

SPORT SCHOOL IS CHANGING SCOTTISH EDUCATION FOR EVER

What is the essence of school PE to you? Trudging through the icy mud of the cross-country track on a wet winter morning? Shimmying up and down the wall bars until your hands ache? Perhaps it might be something as simple as an opportunity to play tennis, football or hockey in the playground. But elite sports development? Doubtful.

Not everyone's school PE career is particularly distinguished, nor do we all have overly fond memories of the mandatory gym time. But what would certainly make PE more worthwhile would be if there were quality facilities (no more cold showers) and equipment, highly trained teachers, well-structured classes and the opportunity to improve in your sport, every single lesson.

An impossible dream? For many of us, perhaps. But not for a selection of lucky youngsters in Glasgow. For them, every day is PE day. Every day, they play their favourite sport. And every day they get that little bit better. One day, they may even represent their country. At least, that's the plan. Because they are the lucky pupils of the Glasgow School of Sport at Bellahouston Academy, Scotland and Britain's first school dedicated to sporting excellence.

The logic is simple. The school has five core sports — athletics, badminton, gymnastics, hockey and swimming. A panel of experts select Scotland's best young talent in these sports, and take on the responsibility of ensuring these children enjoy an education in their sport that can help take them to the very top in their adulthood.

Scotland isn't quite on a sporting par with Australia – yet. But there are little pockets of excellence dotted around Scotland that like to defy the conventional culture that has held us back for so long. Everywhere you look, there are exceptions to the rule that say, 'it doesn't have to be like that': people who dare to be.

For example, it is said in sport that to compete on the world stage, it takes around 10,000 hours of practice and preparation. In bite-size portions, that's 500 hours a year for 20 years – amounting to more than 80 minutes a day, every day. And if you want to have Sundays off, plus Christmas, New Year, birthdays and a summer holiday, you can add a couple more years of graft in there before you make it to the top.

If you are reading this and you are beyond your early teenage

Pupils follow a balanced curriculum of academic studies, which offers up to 12 hours of high-performance coaching a week. The coaching team comprises 20 coaches, and a sports medicine and sports science programme also underpins each sport.

The school aims to ensure Scotland can compete with and win against the best on the world stage. The school's pupils of today are Scotland's potential heroes of tomorrow. Angie Porter has been Director of the Glasgow School of Sport since its inception in 1999, and she is very proud of the record the school has built in those few years.

'Over 60 of our pupils have represented Scotland, which is a phenomenal amount of youngsters. We have gold and silver medallists from the Commonwealth Youth Games, [swimmers Rebecca Hillis and Charles Mills] and hockey player Kenny Bain was at the Youth Olympics and got a silver medal.'

Indeed, Kenny Bain is widely recognised as being one of the school's star pupils. In the 2007 Euro Hockey Youth Nations Championships held at Peffermill in Edinburgh, Kenny scored ten goals in five games, and came away with the Player of the Tournament award. In 2007 he also won his first Scotland cap at just 16 years old when he was selected to tour to Egypt with the squad.

'Not only is Kenny a high achiever within sport, he is also completely committed to what he does,' explains Angie. 'He understands the relationship between academic life and his sporting career. He is firmly grounded.'

years, you are probably saying to yourself, 'That's my chance out the window then.'

Well, maybe not. There is salvation for those of us who left it too late, or, more likely, were too distracted by other temptations and pleasures to fully commit to an athletic career in our formative years. Just ask Lee McAdam, one of the world's best taekwondo fighters.

Born and raised in Coatbridge, outside Glasgow, Lee had never really taken part in much competitive sport. But then, at the age of 24, Lee and her brother Mark were tempted by a newspaper ad to go along to their local taekwondo club. And she quite enjoyed it. So much so that at the age of 31, she has now competed at two World Championships in the last four years.

That's a pretty impressive turnaround, particularly in view of the fact that when she went to her first World Championships in Korea in 2004, Lee had only gained her black belt the previous week. But Lee isn't unique. She is a champion among champions at her club, which is a hotbed of Scottish, British, European and World Championship medal winners.

Based in St Andrew's Sport Complex, the fighting and medals are only the tip of the iceberg in a sport that has much deeper roots in Coatbridge. Because this isn't only a sports club; it is a community, a school, a home from home. Taekwondo is simply the glue that holds the members together.

'The club is like a wee family,' explains Lee. 'There's a good network of people. We have a good team, and even outside taekwondo we all socialise together. Though there's no drinking – you've got to look after yourself!'

She isn't joking when she refers to the club as family. Lee and her brother Mark form the cornerstone of the Scottish taekwondo team. Her niece, Mark's daughter, Emily, has just finished her kiddies' class, where she enjoyed some expert coaching from Donna Murphy, the club's gold European champion. Donna's father, Davie, is the head coach of both the club and the Scotland men's team. At this club, blood really is thicker than water.

But aside from the family values of the club, what is it about taekwondo itself that so compelled late-starter Lee?

'I like all the different aspects of it – the training side, the self-defence and the competition. Not all martial arts have that.' Poignantly, the three traits that come from these aspects are what make a sport like taekwondo so valuable in everyday life. With training comes self-discipline, with self-defence comes self-respect and with competition comes respect for others – a pretty solid foundation for any athlete to build on, and perhaps an insight into why Lee managed to develop into a world-class fighter so quickly.

Coatbridge may seem an unlikely breeding ground for sporting champions, but, amazingly, there is one area in Scotland that has produced more world-class athletes than any other in the entire United

Kingdom, and that is official. With a population of just 13,500 people, the district of Badenoch and Strathspey has produced more Olympians per head of the population – 14 – than any other area in Britain, including silver medallist Craig MacLean (cycling, 2000) and bronze medallist Alain Baxter (skiing, 2002).

Snowboarder Lesley McKenna, who has represented Great Britain at the Winter Olympics in 2002 (Salt Lake City) and 2006 (Turin), is another of the area's 'famous fourteen'. She is Britain's most successful snowboarder ever, and is one of the best in the world at her event, the halfpipe. But things could have been very different for Lesley, had she gone down the route of settling for what she had, rather than having the ambition to aim higher. As a young athlete in her teens in the mid-'90s, Lesley actually started out her sporting career as a skier. She had been on the British and Scottish downhill ski teams for several years. But even at a young age she felt as if things were always going against her.

'It was a really difficult time because I had no money at all and I had to work about five jobs to fund my skiing. I literally worked all the time. I worked as a waitress, in a bar, taught aerobics and cleaned. I did everything I could whenever I wasn't on snow to make ends meet, as well as train four hours a day.

'That wasn't what broke me, though. What broke me was that nobody seemed to have any belief. When I said to everyone that I was going to be a really successful ski racer, and I was going to win a world cup, my collective support network didn't believe in me. A lot of it was down to the fact that they were having massive trouble trying to see how anybody could do anything with the funds they had. They were the ones who were doing the budgets. When you're 21, you don't know anything about budgets, but you can feel when someone's heart isn't really in it.'

Rather than get dragged down, Lesley decided to take a drastic step that changed her life and her career.

'All my friends in Aviemore were snowboarders, I went up with them every day, and they were trying to get me to change to snowboarding. They made a bet with me that they could get me the same sponsorship for snowboarding as I had for skiing.

'But it wasn't so much their bet that spurred me on, it was their belief that I could be a very successful snowboarder that made me take the risk. They were a bunch of people who were prepared to dream a little bit, and they realised how hard I worked to get there. It was the attitude that made me change. It was them loving their sport, for the pure love of it, not for anything else. I knew this was where I belonged.

'I don't react very well to people that are not passionate. The minute things are pinned down, and I'm not allowed to take risks, then that's the minute that everything goes wrong for me. I'm not sure where that comes from, but maybe it's because I've always had to take big risks to get to where I have got to. I've always been the underdog, and there's probably a little bit of a mentality there. You have to be focused and determined and know which way you want to work. I was pretty stubborn and I would stick to my guns.'

McKenna dared to be different. So must Scotland. So must you.

HOW WE CREATE A CULTURE OF WINNING IN SCOTLAND . . .

- Aim higher: go for the win, and don't be scared of losing. Even the best in the world lose sometimes. The higher you aim, the further you go.

- Compete more: the more you test yourself, and the harder the opposition, the sooner you will improve.

- Appreciate all of Scotland's winners: we have champions in so many sports. We should celebrate them, and demand that they receive better recognition.

- Dare to be: don't be afraid to try something new; being different is what has made so many successful Scots who they are today.

7

FIT FOR LIFE

PART I

EAT WELL TO LIVE WELL

THE GOOD OLD DAYS – FISH AND CHIPS FOR WINNERS!

Ask Allan Wells, Scotland's Olympic sprint gold medallist, who is his hero, and he answers, 'That's easy, it was Alf Tupper.' Walter Smith also remembers Alf with considerable affection and enjoyed reading about his exploits.

So who was Alf Tupper? Was he a long-forgotten Scottish runner from the 1950s? Well, sort of. Alf Tupper was the cartoon-strip creation from *The Rover* and *The Victor* weekly comics, which were a mixture of gritty Second World War stories, derring-do and sporting tales, produced by DC Thomson in Dundee. Alf Tupper was a legend. He was known as the 'Tough of the Track'. He worked as a welder and he was always late for training and late for his races, and he lived on a diet of fish and chips, which he devoured with great gusto after every athletics meet. He hung up his spikes in 1992, after beating a generation of toffee-nosed Oxbridge types.

We can look at Alf Tupper's diet and say that there was some merit in what he ate. The fish was good – although it was in batter – and the potatoes, although dipped in animal fat, were also highly nutritious, if he had been burning up calories in a race. And as long as Alf had some green vegetables and resisted extra-sugary sweets and drinks, then he was going to be fine. It didn't do Alf any harm.

What to eat, when and why, is a real issue for young athletes today. Unfortunately, the mainstream diet in Scotland is not really suitable if you want to perform as a winner. And eating properly has to become a lifestyle choice that you adopt – and then stick with.

Scotland has an obesity problem. We're one of the fattest nations on earth, not a record we should be keen to retain. Unfortunately, this problem is apparent from Primary One – and it has been getting worse. Too many young Scots are desperately overweight and this can store up future problems such as heart disease, colon cancer, stomach cancer, breast cancer, diabetes, arthritis, high blood pressure, infertility and strokes. And it is our present generation who might end up paying for all of this future ill-heath. Not great, is it?

Most young people today have been brought up in the era of fast food – with burgers, French fries, pizza, fizzy drinks, crisps and ice cream decorated with thick chocolate sauces. Our parents must take some of the blame. They thought they were spoiling us by taking us out for a Happy Meal at a burger chain. But the legacy has made many people unhappy and dissatisfied with their appearance.

Of course, the occasional cheeseburger and chips isn't necessarily bad, but a generation of young Scots have been consuming far too much sugar, salt and fat. Eating fast food when out for the day, then junk food back at home lounging in front of the television, is not the diet of a winner.

Obesity is extremely difficult to cure: during the thousands of years when food was scarce, human beings developed physiological mechanisms which were very efficient when it came to storing energy as fat. Until the last 25 years, there were very few nations in the world which enjoyed an over-abundance of cheap food. As a result, our bodies are far more efficient at gaining weight than at losing it.

THE NEW GENERATION

It's only recently that health officials have realised that prevention is better than having liposuction treatment to suck out the layers of white fat from your stomach. And sport – and striving to be a winner – plays an important part in this prevention. One of the benefits of taking part in active sport is that it burns the fat off.

The first thing to recognise is that being a winner doesn't entail an expensive diet. A winning diet means eating a balance of good, healthy foods; this could be meat, chicken, fish, fruit and vegetables, and cutting out the extra carbohydrates, sugar and fizzy drinks that we consume during the day.

Walter Smith, the Rangers manager, talks about how a footballer's diet has changed over the years.

'One of the developments that I have noticed in football management has been the advancement of sports science – and nutrition is a big part of this. It has made an enormous difference to the overall fitness of our professional football players.'

You don't see many pot-bellied professional footballers or rugby players any more.

'Our diet, especially in Scotland, is something that everyone needs to be aware of throughout their lives,' continues Smith. 'Thankfully, everyone seems to be more aware of that now. A lot of the time people have been saying, "It's OK to buy these nice foods, if you can afford it." But what I see about the diets that the sports science lads bring in for professional footballers is they are not filled with expensive foods; they're filled with very basic foods that are made in the right way.

'I've noticed an enormous difference in their diet and their training regimes and levels of fitness over the years. The game of football is far faster – and that applies to most sports – and the more you pay attention to diet and fitness regimes, the more you are able to run faster for longer. And that's what football is about.'

So there it is: *very basic foods that are made in the right way.*

THIS ISN'T A DIET PLAN, BUT ...

This chapter isn't about giving you a diet plan – it's about getting you to think about what you put in your mouth. This means thinking about your potatoes – baked or boiled but not deep-fried in lard.

It also means thinking about fresh vegetables – that's more carrots, broccoli, Brussels sprouts, cauliflower, green beans – and fruit – apples, oranges, bananas, pears and grapes – rather than living off pre-cooked and pre-packaged meals that have been in the deep freeze for three months. Your body needs a proper balance of nutrients and energy to allow it to perform at its peak.

Of course, today we are bombarded with the celebrity chefs, such as Jamie Oliver and Scotland's own Gordon Ramsay (who played for Rangers, runs marathons and likes showing off his pecs) explaining how to cook good food. What they are telling us, in a highly entertaining way, makes a lot of sense. Simple food that is well prepared is tasty and good for you.

This is echoed by Irene Riach, the Performance Nutritionist at the Scottish Institute of Sport. Having spent ten years with Celtic FC before joining the Institute, and also regularly acting as a consultant to several English Premiership clubs, Irene has advised hundreds of top athletes across a wide range of sports on what they should be eating to ensure that they perform to their peak. But whether you are a sprint cyclist, a squash player or just a dog-walker, the key messages remain the same with regard to diet.

'It is generally recognised that nutrition has a key role to play in athletic performance as well as general health,' says Irene. 'However, advice can be confusing. The press says that scientists always change their minds or that advice is contradictory. However, the basic concepts of good nutrition have remained strong for many years now.'

IRENE'S ADVICE: ENERGY FOR HEALTH AND EXERCISE

A healthy, well-balanced diet must contain the correct amounts of essential nutrients and provide adequate energy.

TO BE A HIGH-PERFORMANCE ATHLETE, YOU MUST BE A HIGH-PERFORMANCE PERSON, SAYS CHRIS CUSITER

Scotland and British Lions rugby star Chris Cusiter is a high-performance athlete. His job, as a scrum-half, involves foraging for the ball, scampering from one side of the pitch to the other and making pin-point kicks and passes for the players around him. Here's how Chris stays on top of things off the pitch to ensure he is as sharp as possible on it.

'Professional rugby is a lifestyle rather than just a job,' says Chris. 'You don't do a nine-to-five job and then go home and do whatever you want. It is a lifestyle that determines what you do after training, what you eat, how you spend your downtime, your social life and your rest time.

'How you choose to do that is something that comes from within. I think you should treat each player as an individual, but personally I feel a responsibility to do what I feel is best for my rugby. There are times when you get a little break, and it is nice to switch off, but generally you are focused on your performance. Your training is sculpted to get you towards that game. But you have to train your body to get the best out of it. You can't go out too much or be too active outside of rugby.

'It has almost become the norm for me. I lived with a couple of guys who aren't pro players, and the difference in lifestyle is quite notable. It's just the way it has to be if you want to play professional sport. You have to sacrifice things. There are times when you need to relax but generally you have to be very strict with yourself.

'I think you have to take a reality check every now and again. A lot of people want to be professional rugby players, but not everyone can. If it's a possibility, then you have to have the right combination of ability and work ethic, and then you might have the chance of making it to the next level. I was very focused on my rugby.'

CARBS

Victoria Beckham and the rest of the WAGs may be on a low-carb diet, but in terms of providing the body with healthy fuel, most of your calorie intake, about 60–70 per cent, should come from carbohydrates, with protein taking up 15–20 per cent and fat 15–20 per cent. In terms of the amount of energy or calories in each fuel-type, fat provides more than double the calories per gram than carbohydrates, giving 9kcals per gram, whereas carbohydrate and protein give you 4kcals per gram.

Carbohydrates – or carbs – are the most important fuel for the working muscles, and they should make up the bulk of your diet. Carbs can be classified into two groups: sugars (simple carbohydrates) and starches (complex carbohydrates). Simple carbohydrates are sweets, sugar, glucose drinks (like Lucozade), cakes and pastries. They provide an immediate burst of energy, while complex carbohydrates such as potatoes, rice, pasta, vegetables, grains and pulses release their energy over a longer period of time.

Carbohydrates are so important in sports performance because they are a limited source of readily available fuel, which is stored in the muscles, circulating in your bloodstream and in your liver as glycogen. The average person has approximately 2,000kcals of energy stored in their muscles. When this limited source of energy becomes depleted, it is often referred to as 'hitting the wall' or the 'knock'.

In endurance sports like running and cycling, you can spare some of your muscle glycogen by providing an additional readily available energy source such as a carbohydrate drink or high carbohydrate snacks.

If you are exercising regularly, and planning on several consecutive days of training or activity, you should increase your carbohydrate intake in order to keep your muscles well fuelled and allow good recovery.

DIETARY FATS

Fat is also essential for a balanced diet. As well as providing energy, it provides a medium for allowing various micronutrients into the body. Unlike glycogen, fat storage is not a limiting factor for exercise. Even the leanest of athletes has a large reserve of fat for energy, so there is no need to consume a lot of fat. You should be aiming for around 15–20 per cent of your dietary energy to be from fat. A low-fat, high-carbohydrate diet is best for both health and performance.

Of your fat intake, the proportion of poly- and mono-unsaturated fat (sunflower and olive oils, raw nuts and seeds and their oils, and oily fish) should be higher than saturated fats (processed meats, cakes, biscuits, pastries and fried foods). You should also be aware of the 'hidden' fats in your diet, as these are often saturated (e.g. creamy and buttery sauces, mayonnaise-type dressings, pastries, cheesy foods and the above-mentioned foods). Avoid hydrogenated fats, as these are chemically altered and behave just like saturated fats in the body, and are again found in processed foods and many convenience meals.

PROTEIN

Protein is made up of smaller building blocks called amino acids, some of which can be manufactured by the body, and some of which are essential and must be provided by dietary sources. Good sources of protein are meat, fish, dairy produce, seafood, tofu, eggs, soya, Quorn and pulses. Protein increases the rate at which your muscles repair and grow.

FRUIT AND VEGETABLES

Scientific research to date illustrates that populations with higher fruit and vegetable consumption tend to have lower rates of heart disease, strokes and many cancers. The exact reason is not clear but higher consumption is positively linked.

The current recommendations are to consume at least five portions, or a daily total of 400g, of fruit and vegetables. It is important to try to eat a 'rainbow' of colours to ensure you receive a variety of nutrients. If you compare Scotland's average intake of around three portions to that of our continental counterparts, who consume an average of eight portions, we have a long road to travel.

DO WE NEED SUPPLEMENTS?

Over the last few years, there has been much in the press on supplements, both for health and also in sport. Within the performance environment, athletes are subject to rigorous doping controls, and as such there have been some positive drug tests where supplement usage has been implicated. In 2003, independent research highlighted concerns of supplements being contaminated with 'banned' substances. Athletes are very aware of the dangers of contamination, and the industry has gone to great lengths to tighten up quality control procedures.

EVERY DAY IS A TRAINING DAY TO REACH THE TOP, SAYS MODERN PENTATHLETE MHAIRI SPENCE

Three basics play a large part in your life if you want to be a winner: a healthy diet, avoiding injury and getting enough sleep. For this, you need balance and a routine in your life that suits your lifestyle. Modern pentathlete Mhairi Spence, from Inverness, knows all about trying to keep a balance. As well as trying to master five different sports — swimming, running, pistol-shooting, fencing and horse-riding — to Olympic standard, she is also studying for a degree! So how does she do it?

'Although I am still at university, it is pretty much like a full-time job. I come to university at 8 a.m. and I probably leave at 6 or 7 p.m. I do different sessions, trying to fit everything in. It just takes time to get a good balance between social life and training. To start with, it was very hard; as a student, I wanted to do student things. But it's getting the balance right that's important. The reason I came here was to train, so that's my number one priority.

'As you mature as an athlete, you find a balance and a routine which makes it a lot easier. When I first started, I got thrown in at the deep end, and you do struggle through the few first months or so, then it becomes second nature. It's normal now for me to get up in the morning and train. I don't take a day off unless I am sick.

'It would be lying to say I don't dread training some mornings, especially if I'm tired. I think everyone is the same, no matter what you do. Even if you are living the dream, I am sure there will be days when you want to curl up and go back to sleep, but 90 per cent of the time I enjoy training.'

However, for the average population a good balanced diet will suffice to meet requirements. Some circumstances may warrant supplementation under strict supervision (for instance, rugby players often use protein supplements such as creatine or instant whey protein shakes to help increase their muscle mass), but it will always remain an athlete's sole responsibility to remain drug free.

Unfortunately, athletes do sometimes break the rules and use illegal drugs to improve their performance. High-profile cases in recent years have been British sprinter Dwain Chambers and American athlete Marion Jones. Chambers tested positive for the banned anabolic steroid

THG in 2003, while Jones, in October 2007, admitted to taking steroids at the 2000 Sydney Olympics (where she won five medals). Both were banned from Olympic participation, stripped of their medals and widely condemned by their peers and the general public.

SCOTLAND'S WINNING FLAVOUR

We are very fortunate to have such a wide variety of home produce in Scotland. Yes, we are known for our deep-fried Mars Bars and haggis, but we also have fantastic fresh ingredients on our doorstep.

In fancy restaurants throughout the world, diners will pay top dollar for our produce, such as Scottish salmon, wild venison, Aberdeen Angus beef, Scotch lamb, Musselburgh leeks, Arran pilot potatoes and Perthshire strawberries and raspberries, to name but a few!

So get out there, support our local farmers and eat fantastically fresh, local, healthy produce like seafood, game, beef, lamb, potatoes, vegetables, soft fruit, and not forgetting our porridge oats! They are all highly nutritious, and you will have helped the environment by cutting your food miles.

GETTING YOUR BODY IN TUNE

Now consider Orkney athlete William Sichel, one of the world's most successful ultra-distance runners. Competing in races that can last 24 hours, 48 hours and up to a mammoth six days, when he can cover over 500 miles, William requires a special diet. He has made the study of his own food intake a precise science.

'In ultra running, nutrition is absolutely critical. It doesn't matter how good your basic speed is, how talented you are or what your muscles are like, you do have to take in nutrition,' says Sichel. 'A good marathon runner can get by just on water, but an ultra runner has to take in water, carbohydrate and electrolytes, as the absolute minimum.'

You also have to avoid stomach upsets. Your organs and intestines get jangled around like loose change in your pocket when you run, causing all sorts of problems. Nearly all of William's performances have been affected by this problem.

'I graduated in science, I have a science background, and I used all that knowledge and training to try to work out why I was having difficulties. It has taken 11 years of personal research to get to where I am today. You need to get enough, but not too much.'

For years, he was paying too much attention to scientific data and was overloading, especially with carbohydrates. All the nutritional books said 60 grams of carbohydrate per hour is what you need, but for 90 per cent of ultra runners that is impossible.

'You can't take that in because the body can't process it. I tried to do it in various ways, in liquids, in solids and by combining them,' he says.

And then, about two years ago, doing circuits, he discovered that he could do very well on just 35 grams of carbohydrate an hour and run like a dream.

'And that made me realise that I was different from the textbook athlete. And this is the skill, fine-tuning the nutrition to the individual. Yes, you read the research and look at what the experts are saying, but then you have to apply it to you: your stomach, your physiology. And that does take time.'

As soon as you run a step your body is under additional stress – indeed, each step must take two and a half times your body weight. That's a considerable stress load over a concerted period of intense activity. It's a matter of trying to find a formula that works for you. Unfortunately, there is no book on the shelf that will tell you all this: it comes from experience and feedback.

For example, a race doctor in Holland suggested to William that he might be suffering from acid accumulation in his stomach.

'I was absolutely dumbfounded, because I had never heard it mentioned in all that literature I had read. When the body gets excited or stressed, one of its reactions is to produce a lot of acid.'

How did he counteract it?

'You have to buffer the acid. In a normal situation, you just need to have some solid food or an antacid tablet. But I am one of those who can't really assimilate solid food in races; my body doesn't like to use the energy digesting it.

'So a step forward I have made is adding sodium bicarbonate to my drink. Most sports drinks are quite acidic, they are pH 4 or 5, because of the added flavouring. I now add sodium bicarbonate to raise the pH to about 8, and the alkalinity buffers the stomach acid.'

So while William is certainly an extreme, his case sends out a strong message about nutrition. What matters to winners is to eat and drink properly for your sport.

RAISE THE BAR HIGH OR DRINK THE BAR DRY?

The science of hydration is now an essential part of a winning athlete's make-up. Water is the key to this. All sportspeople should aim to replace the fluid used up during sporting activity, and water is by far the best in 90 per cent of cases. However, there are times when taking in water might also flush out essential nutrients that you need for energy, so a fruit or isotonic sports drink might be better during a long and arduous training session. One thing is also clear: alcohol and high performance don't mix. Today, more top athletes are giving up – or at least cutting back – their alcohol consumption. And it goes without saying that smoking is a very foolish habit for anyone who wants to take their sport, and themselves, seriously.

Even professional rugby players, who traditionally might have enjoyed a few beers after a Saturday game, are turning teetotal. Now this is a moot point, because having a drink after a sporting occasion is part of the joy of taking part. While 'everything in moderation' is a wonderful adage for those happy to bump along, total abstinence from anything that will damage a top performance, at least in the run-up to the event, is one of the traits of an elite winner. Just ask Ally Hogg, one of Scotland's top young players and captain of Edinburgh Rugby.

'When all my mates were going out drinking, I was in the gym training and playing games at the weekend, so I couldn't go out. But it was definitely worth it. I wouldn't be here doing what I'm doing now if it wasn't for the sacrifices I made. I could have gone out and got pissed instead of training, but you have to make those sacrifices; that's just the way it is, like in any other job. You knew what the right decision was; you just had to make it. Luckily, it has paid off. I could have done all that and not gone anywhere, but I really enjoyed it, so it wasn't difficult.

You could still go out and just not drink. It was just one of those things you have to do to get where you are, and that's it really.'

Susie Elms, the Performance Lifestyle Coordinator at the Scottish Institute of Sport, who has helped a number of Scotland's elite athletes, says winning sportsmen and women must try and live like normal people.

'They need to manage the everyday distractions around them, but away from the sport – which is their job – it is important to lead a normal life with family and friends.'

If that involves the occasional glass of wine to unwind, then that should be allowed.

Winners also learn how to read their own bodies. They know how to work out when they are reaching exhaustion. Mike Blair, the Scottish rugby captain against Ireland in the RBS 6 Nations in February 2008, talked about the increase in the speed of the game. The Scots needed to play faster and quicker to beat a talented Irish side. Blair said: 'I measure how fast we are playing by how tired I feel, and I was blowing after 20 minutes. That shows me we can play at a tempo to challenge.'

PART II

GET YOURSELF FIT

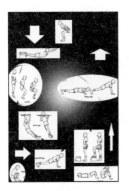

THREE STEPS TO FITNESS WITH TOMMY BOYLE

Leading coach Tommy Boyle, who took Scottish runners Tom McKean and Yvonne Murray to the pinnacle of the international athletics world, says to maintain or improve your general fitness, you only need to worry about three simple forms of work-out:

- Steady Runs
- Circuit Training
- Extensive Interval Training

STEADY RUNS

These form the foundation of aerobic conditioning for many sports. The guidelines are simple: go out for an easy run over a flat course – try to find a loop which takes about 25 minutes – and just build it up very slowly. It is not about beating your times, just covering the distance. Try to establish two or three of these in your weekly life pattern and enjoy!

CIRCUIT TRAINING

If you don't already know, circuit training is where you perform a variety of different exercises, for a set number of repetitions, and build up the volume. Circuit training improves all-round physical fitness, as opposed to fitness for a specific sport. It can be done with little or no equipment and can be done at home, or in a group situation at any hall or centre.

Here's a basic circuit to follow. This will improve your muscular endurance and your explosive strength. Start with a simple group of exercises that use different muscle groups. Do the exercise for a set time, take a recovery and then move to the next exercise. Complete a circuit then repeat the circuit and gradually build up the volume as your fitness improves.

It isn't prescriptive, so you can alter the intensity to suit your own level; change the exercises, add more, take some away, reduce or increase the time. Make sure to stretch and warm up thoroughly.

Exercises

Twenty seconds' effort followed by 20 seconds' recovery – increase to 25 seconds then 30 seconds.

- Calf-raise – stand feet shoulder-width apart, push up on your tiptoes, hold two seconds

- Squats – standing feet shoulder-width apart, squat down until your knees bend at right angles, and back up

- Press-ups – on the floor, hands tight to shoulders, press up to straight arms and back to floor

- Sit-ups – keep your feet on the ground and arms crossed on your chest

- Back-arch – lying in press-up position, keep hips on floor and straighten your arms, hold two seconds then down again

- Squat-jumps – standing on the spot, jump up and tuck both knees in towards your chest

- High-knees running on the spot – pump the arms as if sprinting

- Jog easy on the spot – easy breathing.

EXTENSIVE INTERVAL TRAINING

Here's a rough guide to extensive interval training. This is all about improving your aerobic and strength endurance fitness. The key, says Tommy, is to increase the volume and cut the recovery between efforts, and finally increase speed and recovery as you progress.

Run at about 85 to 90 per cent of your maximum pace – basically a faster rate than your longer runs, at least once per week.

Session 1:

Two sets of 3 x two-minute runs, with two minutes' recovery jogging. Rest for ten minutes between sets.

Session 2:

Two sets of 3 x two-and-a-half-minute runs, with two minutes' recovery jogging. Rest for ten minutes between sets.

Session 3:

Two sets of 3 x three-minute runs, with two minutes' recovery. Rest for ten minutes between sets.

Session 4:

Two sets of 3 x three-minute runs, with 90 seconds' recovery. Rest for ten minutes between sets.

Session 5:

You then start to cover a further distance in the three minutes.

Continue this routine for about six weeks, gradually increasing the run time and reducing the recovery time. Then, once six weeks has passed, you can add a third set, or you may choose to go faster, in which case you then start to increase the recovery again. You can make the session more exciting by doing varied distance sets.

WARMING UP AND PREPARING FOR ACTION, WITH GREGOR TOWNSEND

Former Scotland rugby star Gregor Townsend spent 12 years in the thick of the action as a professional athlete. In such an intense, vigorous sport, it was absolutely fundamental for Gregor to make sure he was properly stretched and loosened up before a big game. Here's his guide to pre-match preparation.

'I always used to go out ten minutes before everyone else on match day to do my own warm-up. Here's my unexciting (but effective) routine . . .'

- Slow jog for about 400 metres – or twice round half a football or rugby pitch.

- Do some back stretches – lie on your back, bend your knees to your chest but keep your feet touching the ground, and move from side to side, then roll back and forward, holding your knees to your chest.

- Back to running – this time some short shuttles, a bit faster, about 20 metres back and forth for 200 metres.

- Do some basic plyometric drills (see below) isolating different parts of the legs:

    1. 2 x 20-metre shuttles of heel-flicks (for hamstrings) followed by a 20-metre jog

    2. Same distance for high-knees (for quads)

    3. Same again side-skips (for adductors)

    4. And again Russian-kicks – that's straight leg running landing on your heels

    5. I finish with high-skips, which is the most explosive drill in the warm-up

- I then do leg swings – leaning on a team-mate or goal post.

- By then my legs are fairly warmed up, so I do two or three 20-metre sprints to finish.

PART III

THE NEW R 'N' R –
RECOVERY AND REHABILITATION

SCOTLAND'S TOP DOCS

More people taking part in sport also means more injury, but you should never let this put you off. All sports fans are shocked when they see events such as the collapse and death of Phil O'Donnell, the Motherwell football captain; or Henrik Larsson's sickening broken leg when playing for Celtic; or an unconscious Rory Lamont, the Scottish rugby winger, being stretchered off with a fractured face in the Calcutta Cup in 2008. Even Andy Murray's famous wrist injury before Wimbledon in 2007 created a pressure on one of Scotland's top athletes to return to the sporting arena as quickly as possible.

Dr John MacLean is the Chief Executive and Medical Director of the National Stadium Sports & Health Clinic at Hampden. He has a job that many people would envy. He's been to the World Cup with Scotland's footballers, looking after their health and wellbeing. He's been on the sidelines of many of Scotland's prize moments working with players of every age level – including the under-16 world championship final in 1989 when Scotland's young blades were pipped by Saudi Arabia in front of 80,000 at Hampden Park. But John doesn't get his tickets for nothing – he is working hard. He has to deal with the wounded and the easing of pain and injury.

'Yes, it sounds like a glamorous job rubbing shoulders with Scotland's best players. But it is non-stop from the minute a campaign trip starts, looking after the players and keeping them match prepared and fit to perform. Then during a match there is always the fear of one of the athletes being hurt and injured.'

John also works closely with Dr Brian Walker, who is Head of Sports

Medicine at the Scottish Institute of Sport, in Stirling, and also team doctor for the Scotland under-19 rugby squad. These two highly experienced doctors work alongside teams of sports physiotherapists, sports medicine scientists and other medical professionals to help athletes recover from injury and improve their performances. Both are at the forefront of sport injury work in Scotland and they have seen a transformation of diagnoses, treatment and rehabilitation over the last 20 years.

This is reassuring for anyone who takes part in sport in Scotland. And anyone who has been involved in a sporting injury can be referred to Dr MacLean's clinic in Glasgow, although increasingly there are experts throughout Scotland, with more GPs in the National Health Service now aware of how to treat specific sports injuries. It is a growing field of expertise: in 1960 just over 1 per cent of admissions to NHS hospital accident and emergency units were caused by sport or leisure activity; in 2000 that figure was over 10 per cent. It's been rising since then and there are 20 million sports-related injuries a year in the UK, costing £1 billion in treatment and people off work.

THE ODDS ARE ON YOUR SIDE

So what are the serious risks of taking part in sport? It should be said first and foremost that taking part enhances the physical wellbeing and all-round fitness of 99.9 per cent of people taking active exercise. There are around 160 deaths a year from sports in Scotland – around 1.3 per cent of all accidental deaths – and those are normally extreme sports involving height, water and speed. There is no doubt that airborne sports, such as hang-gliding and parachuting, mountaineering, and motor sports, including rally driving and motorbike racing, carry the biggest danger of death.

In Scotland, around 75 young people die each year of heart failure – and often the unfortunate person has a history of family cardiac problems. For those taking part and witnessing the collapse of a player, and for the family, the death of a young healthy sportsperson is a personal tragedy.

The death of Motherwell captain Phil O'Donnell in a Scottish Premier League game against Dundee United on 29 December 2007 at Fir Park was heartbreaking for his family and for all football supporters.

LEADING FROM THE FRONT:
Scotland's greatest female runner Liz
McColgan won countless medals in
her glittering career. But she says
all that mattered was being the best
– which in her case was the fastest –
she could be. (© Getty Images)

WINNING TEAM: Rangers
manager Walter Smith (centre)
– flanked by Ally McCoist (left)
and Kenny McDowall (right)
– says successful teamwork
depends on all players striving to
reach a common goal.
(courtesy of Rangers FC)

CAPTAIN FANTASTIC:
Scotland hockey captain
Graham Moodie maintains
that keeping fit and looking
after your body when
sidelined are two of the
most important aspects of a
speedy recovery. (courtesy of
Steve Lindridge, Ideal Images)

WINNING FORMULA: Three-time World Formula One champion Sir Jackie Stewart says it was teamwork by the racing-car crew in the pits that made his success possible. (© Getty Images)

MONTY MAGIC: Colin Montgomerie's ability to raise the spirits of his fellow Ryder Cup team-mates was pivotal in their 2004 win over the USA team at Oakland Hills.
(© Getty Images)

ICE QUEENS: Scottish curlers Margaret Morton, Debbie Knox, capt. Rhona Martin, Janice Rankin and Fiona MacDonald pose with their gold medals at the 2002 Salt Lake City Winter Olympic Games in Utah, USA. (© Getty Images)

FITNESS FANATIC: Alain Baxter is one of Scotland's most gifted athletes, playing shinty and ice hockey to a high level as well as being a professional skier. (courtesy of Snowsport GB)

GET A KICK OUT OF LIFE: Chris Paterson, Scotland's most capped rugby player and record points scorer, says that trying your hardest to be the best is a sure-fire way of achieving your goals. (courtesy of SWpix, SRU)

LEARNING FROM THE BEST: Craig Wright went to Australia to hone his cricket skills and soak up their culture of winning in sport. He led Scotland at the World Cup in 2007 and played against the mighty Aussies. (courtesy of Ian Jacobs, Cricket Scotland)

THE INCREDIBLE ULTRA-MAN: Orkney's William Sichel, multiple ultra-distance-running record holder, fine-tunes his diet to fit the needs of his arduous event, which can involve running over 20 marathons in the space of six days. (courtesy of Alan Young)

DREAM BOY: As a 12 year old, Mark Beaumont set his sights on riding from Land's End to John o'Groats. His ambition led to the massive challenge of cycling around the world in 194 days. Here he is pictured in Lahore, India, during his record-breaking feat. (courtesy of Mark Beaumont)

Topsy-turvy world: Lesley McKenna made the brave decision to switch from skiing to snowboarding at a crucial stage in her career. She was broke and had to persevere through some tough times, but she pursued her dream and became the top snowboarder in the UK. (courtesy of JDP Freelance Photography, Snowsport GB)

FORWARD THINKING: Edinburgh rugby captain and Scotland international
Ally Hogg chose to hit the gym when the rest of his mates went out
drinking. He says the extra work he put in paid off in his bid to become
a better professional. (courtesy of SWpix, SRU)

BOYLE'S LAW: Tommy Boyle, coach to top
Scottish runners Yvonne Murray and Tom
McKean, adopts a coaching philosophy based
upon a scientific knowledge of sport combined
with the common sense and passion to motivate
people. (courtesy of Steve Lindridge, Ideal Images,
Winning Scotland Foundation)

EVERYDAY WINNER: Frank Dick, pictured coaching
Olympic champion Denise Lewis, teaches that the
key to being a winner is in striving to be better every
day. His favourite acronym to achieve this is ODD:
'Own, Decide, Do'. (© Getty Images)

STEERING GROUP:
Chris Hutchens and
Ruaridh Cunningham
at the World Mountain
Bike Championships in
2007; both riders recognise
the importance of time
spent with their coach
and mentor Chris Ball.
(courtesy of Pamela Gilfillan)

HIGH-PERFORMANCE PERSON: British Lions and Scotland rugby star Chris Cusiter believes that he must respect and train his body to ensure he can compete at the highest level. (courtesy of SWpix, SRU)

RAISING THE BAR: World and Olympic champion cyclist Chris Hoy endures another tough lifting session under the watchful eye of Dave Clark, Head of Strength and Conditioning at the Scottish Institute of Sport in Stirling. (courtesy of Scottish Institute of Sport, Steve Lindridge, Ideal Images)

WINNER TAKES ALL: Manchester United manager Sir Alex Ferguson celebrates his second Champions League final victory in 2008. He believes taking part in sport sets a powerful example of how to conduct your life.
(© Getty Images)

THE BIGGEST INJURY STORY OF 2007

Andy Murray's injured wrist in May 2007 in Hamburg was one of the most high-profile injuries of the year in British sport, forcing him to miss Wimbledon, leaving his thousands of fans on 'Murray Mound' devastated. We asked him how he dealt with such an injury.

How did you maintain your speed, agility and alertness while out of action?

Given it was my wrist, I could keep working out with the rest of my body during my injury. I spent a lot of time in the gym and did a lot of cardiovascular work as well as weights and core stability. That helped me get in really good shape.

Did you feel any undue pressure to play at Wimbledon before you were fully recovered? Is this a big pressure for highly paid professionals?

I really wanted to play Wimbledon because it's so great to play in front of the British crowd and get so much support. However, it was more important to be 100 per cent healed of the injury and not run the risk of injuring my wrist further.

What was the biggest frustration?

I had started the year so well having reached the top ten and it was frustrating that I couldn't continue at that level and had to wait several months to get back on the tour.

Did you use the time productively to learn about some other aspects of the professional tennis game?

Yes, the training (physical) aspect became the focus and it allowed me to get in the best shape I have ever been.

'The death of Phil was deeply shocking. Here was the sudden collapse of a very fit athlete at 35 years old and a great ambassador for the power of playing sport throughout your life. Yet, in the wider context, the death of a player in such circumstances is an unusual occurrence,' said Dr MacLean.

Over 80 per cent of all non-traumatic sudden deaths in young competitive athletes are a result of congenital cardiac abnormalities – or heart attacks – with more than 40 per cent of these caused by hypertrophic obstructive cardiomyopathy (a bulge in the ventricle that hinders blood flow), which doctors and health boards are doing more to diagnose.

Playing any sport at a high tempo makes people more likely to be injured. And from any health professional's point of view, the most important thing in all sport is your own health – the health of the competitor. For example, in football and rugby, the most common injuries are to the lower leg, head and neck, upper limbs and the knees.

It is also important that you do not do anything that would deliberately harm others. Sport brings out the most extreme human emotions, and this can lead to moments of anxiety and acute stress. When temper is short and tension is high, flare-ups can result in actions which cause injury. This is completely unacceptable. Sport is dangerous enough already – without hotheads adding to the injury lists.

COPING WITH INJURY

No one wants to get hurt, but minor injury in sport is extremely frequent. And because football is the most popular game in Scotland, about half of all young people needing hospital treatment from a sports injury come from taking part in a soccer match. Thankfully, the vast majority of injuries in sport are minor – and most healthy people can shrug them off with the minimum of treatment in a few days.

Dr MacLean explains, 'In contact sports, there are two kinds of injury: extrinsic which can come from poor technique, training errors, poor conditioning and incorrect equipment, and intrinsic which is related to the athlete's own body. They might be overweight or they might be predisposed to diabetes or other ailments, they might even have flat feet which makes running more difficult unless they have proper shoes to correct this.'

Many of these injuries happen while training.

'If you put excessive loads on your body it causes strain. The tissues of the body are capable of withstanding considerable stress: around two to three times your weight goes through your body, even when you are jogging slowly. But untrained tissues that aren't accustomed to such forces won't be able to withstand this and are likely to be injured through overuse.

SEVEN SECRETS TO RECOVERING FROM INJURY

Scotland hockey captain Graham Moodie has seven top tips on how to stay sharp when recovering from injury. He says, 'Staying fit when injured is very specific to the actual injury. However I'd say it's key to focus on what you can do, rather than the limitations which the injury forces on you.'

1. Use the time off as an opportunity to strengthen other areas of your body. If your legs are injured, then it's an ideal opportunity to work on your upper body or core stability, and vice versa if you have an upper body injury.

2. Always do the rehab prescribed by physios and strength and conditioning coaches. This is crucial for strengthening the weakened area and preventing future similar injuries.

3. If an injury prevents you from doing your sport, use the time you would normally be playing to work on rehab and future injury prevention.

4. If your sport requires cardiovascular fitness then there is almost always some 'cv' work you can do when injured, even if it isn't specific to your sport. For example, when I've been injured I've spent a lot of time on the bike, because although it's not specific to hockey, it can still help your general fitness.

5. Rest is crucial for recovery. Although rehab is essential, don't overdo it or push the injured area too far too quickly.

6. Don't come back too early. I have been persuaded to come back and play when I have not fully recovered on a number of occasions and it has always resulted in re-injuring the same area. It is unbelievably frustrating. And finally...

7. Eat the right things and avoid drinking alcohol. Both can have a positive effect on recovery time.

'When deciding how often, how hard and for how long to exercise, you need to consider the impact on your muscles and joints. You always have to build up gradually to avoid injury,' says Dr MacLean.

Poor technique during training can cause 'overuse injuries', with the best-known examples being tennis elbow, and often the repetition of an action with faulty technique results in injury. Good coaching plays a vital role in curbing injuries. While inappropriate equipment such as footwear and headgear can lead to injury, the failure to warm up properly before an event has been responsible for countless athletes being withdrawn at the last minute due to tweaks and strains. This can be heartbreaking for athletes who have trained for four years and then pulled a muscle minutes before the race of their lives.

'The body's tissues, particularly the muscles, respond better to loading when they're warm. The warming-up process should include whole body exercise that increases blood flow to muscles and makes them more responsive. Then at the end of every training session, you should also warm down, bringing your body back down to normal, usually through low intensity activity, followed by stretching exercises,' says Dr MacLean.

Intrinsic injury risk factors include things such as the shape and structure of the major joints. Many joggers and runners have feet that 'pronate', or roll inwards; this, along with weak arches, often contributes to painful lower leg, shin and knee conditions. And being overweight increases the load on muscles, tendons, ligaments and joint structures during weight-bearing activities.

Of course, while injury prevention is possible throughout the warm-up phase, once the game is under way, the adrenalin takes you into challenges and situations that you would normally avoid. This can sometimes result in more serious traumatic sports injuries such as fractures, dislocations, major muscle ligament or tendon injuries.

For example, two footballers are running for a 50–50 ball. The defender slides in to tackle but kicks the attacker's ankle. The attacking player falls over in agony twisting his knee badly. If there is an obvious injury, then there might be tissue damage, which can cause external bleeding, or internal swelling, where there is bleeding internally. But how do you know how bad this is?

Dr Brian Walker, who has been among the first on the pitch to tend to injured rugby players, says that in any sports injury an accurate diagnosis is essential, and that isn't always possible when someone is lying in agony on the grass or AstroTurf.

'On the spot evaluation is essential and immediate treatment can help the healing process. You need to look at the head, neck and chest to ensure that you are not doing anything that might aggravate the injury. Then once you are sure it is not a neck injury, you need to take extreme care moving that person. It's important to listen to the sportsperson – if conscious.'

A trained first-aider attending someone who has been knocked out cold will be thinking ABC – Airways, Breathing and Circulation. If someone is out cold, then you need to get professional assistance as quickly as possible – and don't move the person, who should be kept warm and covered. Sports first aid is a worthwhile skill to have; courses (involving around 16 hours' study) are supported by the national governing bodies of all Scottish sports.

Proper evaluation of injury speeds up recovery, protects from further injury and enhances performance when the person returns to the sport after rest and repair. And for those at the side of a game – PRICES is an acronym to remember:

P   for protection of the injured area to prevent further damage

R   for rest. This means resting the injured part to prevent further irritation

I   for ice. Ice is good for controlling pain, bleeding and swelling

C   for compression. For support and control of swelling

E   for elevation, so as to decrease the bleeding

S   for support for the injured part of the body.

Putting ice over a swollen ankle, for example, can help reduce swelling within the first 24 hours. You should also consider this: don't put ice directly onto the skin. Use a bag of frozen peas or sweetcorn, wrap it in a dish towel, and then lay it up against the swollen area. A player should never go back on the field after a leg or body part has been iced for treatment.

The healing process can take time. Getting back to your sport after injury does require some physical and mental adjustment. To be stuck on the sidelines can be a lonely vigil and depression and anxiety can set in, so having an optimistic frame of mind is a real asset. This is what Ally Hogg said before the 2007 RBS 6 Nations, when he had suffered a couple of injury setbacks:

'I fractured my elbow, came back and then injured the medial ligament in my knee, so that was a bit disappointing, as it led to me missing my first international since I got my first cap. I had played in every game, and that was something I was quite proud of. But hopefully I'll come back a bit stronger, and that's the way you've got to look at it.

'I suppose it is better missing games through injury as opposed to being dropped, but it's still frustrating. However, that's the nature of the sport, and you've just got to get on with it. Luckily, I'm quite an optimistic guy. You've got to look at the positives. I've worked hard in the gym in the last month, and I've worked on some skills. The best way to deal with injury is just to stay positive.

QUICK MICK'S SLOW FIX

Being Britain's top downhill skier, Finlay Mickel has had lots of ups and downs, both on and off the piste. Hurling his body down the side of a mountain at the same speed as a commuter on the M8, the risk of injury is high, and one which caused him to question his career.

'I missed out on the 2002 Olympic Games due to breaking my leg, which was a huge blow. In the following six months off skis, I learned a lot about myself. I had to assess what I was doing and why I was doing it, and ask myself, "Is it all worth it after a bad injury?" I came back with the definite answer that, yes, it is. The time out gave me the chance to realise how much I enjoyed the sport and I put in that extra effort to make the next step, which was when I really started moving into the forefront as a skier making not just the top 30, but the top ten positions at the World Cup.

'I even managed to iron out a few technical issues, due to having to relearn how to walk! I used that to get rid of some old bad habits.'

'When I get injured, I can't play rugby for a while, but I can go and work on my passing or with upper-body weights. Sometimes, it's actually nice to get a bit of a break away from rugby. And it is an opportunity to come back refreshed and come back better. You can do things you wouldn't normally have time to do. For instance, some of the boys take an injury as an opportunity to do some educational stuff, like starting a course.'

Some people naturally heal faster than others. But the amazing news is that injuries that would have been career-threatening 20 years ago are now fixable. For example, British Lions rugby star Simon Taylor and Scotland captain Jason White have been able to return to the game following injuries that would have finished playing careers a generation ago.

More recently, keyhole surgery, rehabilitation techniques and intensive sports physiotherapy have allowed sportspeople to return to training soon after surgery without putting pressure on the recovering area. Damage to the cruciate ligament in the knee and the cartilage is one of the most common injuries in ball sports, though modern techniques – such as ultrasound and the use of removable pneumatic plastic supports rather than plaster of Paris casts – don't always make recovery much faster.

Dr MacLean says, 'I've been asked how long it takes to recover from a knee ligament injury. Twenty years ago, it took six to eight weeks. Today, even with all the latest medical technology, it is still six to eight weeks. We still rely on Mother Nature to heal a wound.'

Another difference today is that extensive physiotherapy and workouts, such as the resistant hydro pool (a treadmill at the bottom of a shallow pool, allowing people with leg injuries to run without the strain of their own body weight), means that players can return to sport as match-fit as possible.

To be a winner, you must be prepared to do the work during recovery to get back to fitness. If you have been seriously injured playing sport, you should always seek the help and advice of a good sports physiotherapist to get you back to normal. In the modern world of competitive sport, a physio's role is crucial towards not just recovery, but general day-to-day conditioning and flexibility. And they do more than just bend your legs back in uncomfortable positions and poke at your injuries, explains Fiona Mather, Head of Physiotherapy at the Scottish Institute of Sport.

'It is really important that the rehabilitation of athletes is multifaceted. When you are actually rehabilitating an injured athlete, it is extremely important to address all aspects of the athlete and not just to think about the injury. For example, the psychology of the injury: if the injury happened on the sports field, when the athlete returns to the field, the injury is in his or her mind all the time.

'I also believe it is key for a physio to understand the demands of the sport. You shouldn't cringe when watching your athletes compete. You should be 100 per cent confident that you have addressed all avenues of rehabilitation.

'If you're worried about someone going back onto the field or into the pool, then you are either not confident in your own skills, or the athlete is not ready to be back there. It's not just about patching people up and throwing them back onto the field.'

The message is that you should resist the temptation to return to the fray before you are properly and fully recovered, something that Andy Murray bore in mind to his benefit after his much publicised injury in 2007.

Fiona's colleague Dr Brian Walker offers one last secret of recovery:

'An injured player needs rest to recover. It is often underestimated, but sleep is a great healer, too. Recuperating players who keep feeling tired and exhausted are often staying up late playing their Xbox or PlayStation. There is no doubt that sleeping is part of recovery, or that the quality of recovery will have a major impact on the quality of performance. Recovery matters.'

The need for rest is also why many coaches impose curfews regarding nightclubs in the run-up to big games!

Alain Baxter, Scotland's most successful skier, recognises the benefits of proper rest and recovery. As a professional skier on the demanding World Cup circuit, Alain has endured many rigorous training sessions, and over the years he has recognised that the key to getting the best from them is giving his body a rest afterwards.

'We do a lot of endurance training, physical work. Around 14 hours per week, two sessions a day of pretty heavy-going stuff. A few years ago, the coaches would drill us into the ground without time to recover, and we would be knackered!

'Now, though, with the advancement of sports science, we have recognised that you can't just train yourself into the ground and be expected to compete at a high level. It's a fine mix, with the coaches and the Scottish Institute of Sport working together on strength and conditioning and other aspects, I think we've got a good base now, a good programme. So we can train and compete without being "totally beat".'

Fitness and health and recovery from injury go hand in hand. From a winner's point of view, getting hurt from time to time is an expected part of the process. There is outstanding expertise, advice and support available throughout Scotland to ensure that sportspeople recover safely and are able to return to the fun and games as soon as possible.

To your good health!

STEPS TO BEING FIT FOR LIFE . . .

- Eat well and enjoy your life: avoid junk food, keep a balanced diet and avoid alcohol and kick out cigarettes. Your mind and body need this to perform at their best.

- Stay fit and healthy: there are so many sports and activities you can do, from the very easy to the near impossible. But as long as your body is getting regular exercise, you're doing well.

- Avoid injury: warm up and cool down well, and don't be rash. If you do get hurt, remember the PRICES acronym to aid your recovery.

- Rest up: get a good night's sleep every night, and give your body and brain the chance to take a break.

THE EXPERTS' OPINION:

DR BRIAN WALKER
HEAD OF SPORTS MEDICINE

Brian is Scotland's first full-time sports doctor. His role at the Institute involves the medical profiling and consulting of athletes, preventing and reducing injury and illness, and contributing sports medicine to the Institute's programmes. Along with the physiotherapy unit, his role is important not just in preventing injury but in improving performance.

'Different people develop at different rates. There are some athletes who, from the very moment you meet them, you know they are going to achieve. But for every one of them there is another who you need to help along. I firmly believe that when I had Chris Cusiter as an under-19, he transformed from a decent rugby player into a British Lion due to his innate drive and energy, and the help he received from some of the guys at the Institute.

'Dealing with injury in the correct manner is vital. There are personality characteristics that allow you to cope with injury, and they do point you in the direction of becoming a champion. There are people with fundamental physical flaws, but managing them is part and parcel of being a winner.

'Being the best athlete means having the best self-discipline. It is overall management of life in general departments that athletes need to work on. That applies to people who don't do sport as well: 95 per cent of afflictions are self-inflicted. If you took away obesity, fags, drink, stress and sex, I would be redundant!'

8

IT'S ALL ABOUT ME
. . . ISN'T IT?

COACHES, MANAGERS, MENTORS AND MOTIVATORS

So you think you're pretty special, do you? You're ready to make the step up to the big time? Maybe you've been skimming your way through this book thinking 'Yep, got that, done that, know about that, no worries. I'm set.'

If that's the case, then good for you, you're well on the way to being a winner. Yes, really. Confidence in your own ability is a good thing and if you've got it, that's great. But it isn't enough. You need help – but don't worry, that isn't a bad thing. Getting help isn't a sign of weakness, it's a sign of intelligence. No one's perfect, everyone needs help with something, so why not follow the example of the best sportsmen and women in the world? There have been very few Olympic medals, world championships, majors and slams won without some assistance.

Willie Wallace didn't fight the English on his own, no matter how much Mel Gibson tries to convince us otherwise. In any sport, business or career, very few survive, let alone succeed, on their own. People need coaches, leaders, managers and mentors. It's as natural as parenting or teaching.

PRACTICE MAKES PERFECTION FOR SCOTLAND'S PERFECT KICKER

Chris Paterson is Scotland's legendary goal-kicker in rugby. He had a perfect 100 per cent record of kicks in the RBS Six Nations in 2008 and in the Rugby World Cup in 2007. Chris is renowned around the world for his ability to win points with his boot. But how did he do this? He reveals his secret to *Be a Winner*.

'I practised every day at school but because lunchtime only lasted an hour, I wanted to kick ten out of ten between the posts from around the field, and I didn't go in until I'd done this. I was more confined by time than hitting the percentage, though. Basically I wanted two things, one to be the best player in the school and two to be the hardest-working player in the school.

'I would practise on my own, which caused a couple of problems, the first being that there's not a lot you can do on your own when rugby is a team game. However, what I could do was practise kicking. Secondly, I was doing something "different" or teacher's-pet-like, which was frowned upon by your classmates. Everyone soon got over it, though, and let me do my own thing. I would mainly kick at goal but also practise punting and closed skills, like kick-offs. I never had a technique or a plan, I just kicked and naturally found what seemed to work best. I can remember the main motivation for doing it was to be the best. I suppose it was a selfish attitude in many ways.

'After secondary school, I played club rugby with Gala and would train three times a week. Each time I trained, I would kick at goal at the end of sessions. Then, when I started playing for Scotland, I'd practise kicking but not as much, because I wasn't

Cyclist Chris Hoy puts much of his success down to mentoring and support from fellow Scot Craig MacLean.

'It definitely helped. There were no sprint coaches in Britain at the time, and we were really just doing it on guesswork. I was fortunate really, as I was quite young. It was much more difficult for Craig, who was older and much faster. I had something to aim for and someone to train with, but he was top of the pile, so he didn't have anyone to stretch him. I was lucky to have Craig there, and I was impressed with how inventive he managed to stay in training.'

Gordon Strachan was a legendary footballer and is now one of Scotland's top football coaches. He learned his trade from the likes kicking regularly for Edinburgh or the national team. This was a mistake, as it meant that when I was asked to kick I was inconsistent. Sometimes I'd kick really well and other times I'd kick poorly, and not knowing the reasons why really got to me.

'This coincided with the Scottish Rugby Union appointing Mick Byrne as their kicking and catching coach. I worked with Mick from October 2001 until May 2005. I can honestly say he is the reason that my kicking improved. He worked with my style and made only little changes over a long period. So, if I were to look at my style as it was in 2001 and in 2008, they would be very different, but the change was so gradual you would hardly notice it month by month. I'd work with Mick around three times a week, but I would kick every day at training for around 35–40 minutes. We'd do a lot of video work, looking at perfect practice. Some of the biggest breakthroughs I had were when I'd watch videos of the kicks.

'Now, I'll kick until I feel happy with my strike. Sometimes that can be five minutes, sometimes an hour. I also try to put my kicks in training into the context of a game, in order to train under pressure. If I'm having a really bad day, I just stop and walk in.

'How did Mick help me? Easy. He educated me, he'd ask me to hold my follow-through or keep my left shoulder over the ball, then he'd tell me why I should do that, and what would happen if I didn't. Over time, Mick allowed me to build up knowledge that allowed me to self-evaluate every kick immediately after the strike. Now, when I kick, I tend to know if it's going over or missing before I look up. Having that knowledge is invaluable when I miss a kick, because I generally know why it missed and what I have to do to correct it.

'My training has changed dramatically since my schooldays, but my attitude hasn't!'

of Alex Ferguson, first at Aberdeen, then with Manchester United. Ferguson himself looked to an older, wiser head for inspiration, when he felt he and his team needed it: he used to play Strachan and his team-mates old tape recordings of Bill Shankly talking. If Strachan can turn to Ferguson, and Ferguson can turn to Shanks, it shows that, even at the very top level, the value of a coach can be immeasurable.

As you can see, no individual, no duo, no team in their right mind would set out to conquer their goals without a coach, a manager or a mentor. And nor should you. Every great winner has an equally great coach or manager behind them. Scotland has got into the habit of producing some of the very, very best in the business: Sir Alex Ferguson,

Ian McGeechan, Sir Matt Busby, Frank Dick, Bill Shankly, Bob Torrance, Tommy Boyle, Walter Smith, Judy Murray and Jock Stein, to name but a few. But coaches come in all forms and at every level; just because you can't get Sir Alex doesn't mean you don't need a coach.

So what can a coach bring to the table? Well, the question you should be asking is 'What can a coach bring to *your* table?' That's the beauty of it – a coach is there to help you with whatever you need. Need some tactical advice? Ask the coach. Not fit enough? Get a coach. Short on motivation? Bring in the coach!

MANAGING YOUR NEEDS

Training for sports like triathlon or duathlon requires endless hours of pounding the pavements, hundreds of miles on the bike and countless laps of the pool. It is a solitary regime, and success in triathlon is ultimately dependent on the singular, insular determination of the competitor: in a race, no one else can decide to quit or make that final push for the win. But there is still room for a coach, as Catriona Morrison, the ITU Long Distance Triathlon bronze medallist, explains:

'My coach, Gordon Crawford, is very good at putting all the different elements of my programme together. As I have to train for three different disciplines, and do strength and conditioning and core work as well, he's very good at taking a step back and slotting it all into my week. Then I can say to him that I'd like to do a bit more of one thing and a bit less of another. It's a two-way relationship.'

Her coach doesn't just offer technical and administrative assistance, as she points out.

'Halfway through the week, when you're physically exhausted and don't want to do the training, it's good to have someone to turn to, to tell you it's OK, that one session isn't going to make the difference between winning and losing. If you need a break, take one. Other times, you will phone up and say, "I'm really tired" and he will say "tough", then you have to get your sorry bum out the door and do it!'

Fraser Cartmell, another elite Scottish triathlete who finished an impressive seventh place in his first ever Ironman 70.3 World

Championships in November 2007, agrees with Catriona. While he also spends a lot of time preparing for competition on his own, he says you can't underestimate the value of a coach.

'I wouldn't want to not be coached, because I prefer being prescribed the stuff to interact with. It's hard to sit down and think what I should do. I want to have a programme and start picking out what works for me. Every person is different, and triathlon is a unique sport because it has three elements and everyone has different strengths within them; it's good to have someone who knows how you operate and Gordon has a good feel for that.'

This is just the role of one coach in one sport, however. A coach can play many roles; in some cases, you may require different people for each of those roles. The key, therefore, is ensuring that your coach – be it a highly priced professional, a volunteer, a friend or a relative – gets the best out of you in the area you need help with. Judy Murray, the tennis performance adviser for the LTA, former Scottish National coach and, of course, mother to top Scots Andy and Jamie, has some sound advice on what you should look for in a coach.

'Whatever the sport, you will have a range of different types of coaches, be they technical, tactical or mental skills coaches, or physical trainers. You need to be sure that you have the right people with the right experience, and also, importantly, that you get on with them, that there is a fit between your personalities.

'Plus, the whole team have to work together and talk to each other. For example, there is no point in the technical coach and the physical coach working in isolation. You absolutely have to marry everything up, so within your team, there needs to be a lead coach coordinating everything. All the information has to go through that person in order to make it work.'

As you can see, then, it isn't always a matter of looking up 'coaches' in the *Yellow Pages*.

Picking a coach is like choosing a car; always ask yourself the question: 'Will this take me where I want to go?' If you want to buy a vehicle to take off-road and over fields and valleys, you wouldn't buy a sports car. Extending the analogy, if you plan to travel long distances at high speeds on motorways, a respectable dealer would suggest you steer clear of a one-litre compact. Likewise with your coach. Are you an athlete on the verge of making it to the top? Well then, find someone with the expertise to take people to the top. Don't pick someone who has only ever worked with kids or lower-level athletes. It also follows that a local amateur football team should aim lower than Craig Levein or Mark McGhee to take the reins.

NEVER GIVE UP – AND BATTLE UNTIL THE VERY LAST MINUTE

Even Frank Dick, one of Scotland's greatest sporting motivators and coach to double Olympic champion decathlete Daley Thompson, needs to draw inspiration from somewhere. And, of course, where better to start than two Scottish legends, Bill Shankly and Alex Ferguson.

'Bill Shankly had a great line when he was working with kids,' says Frank. 'He'd look them in the eye and say: "If you're not sure about this game son, think of it this way ... imagine that every time you touch the ball, it's the most important touch you'll have in your life and you'll get your game right."

'It's that kind of thinking that matters. You're surrounded by moments in the game, and they are yours to use, but you must visit every one of them with excellence, because you don't know when it's going to turn.'

Frank also talks about Sir Alex. He has inspired his teams to fight for every single ball until the final whistle blows – and to never give up.

'Do you remember the last three minutes of the Manchester United versus Bayern Munich game in the Champions League Final in 1999? Manchester United won 2–1 with two goals in the dying minutes. Three minutes of injury time had been added when Beckham's corner was put into the penalty box for Teddy Sheringham to score. Then, less than 30 seconds later, United scored from another corner.

'I've got a bit of video shot by Andy Roxburgh and his technical team from behind the Bayern goal. After United had put in the second goal, there was still about 60 seconds of the game to go. What we all missed on normal television, and what that camera picked up was the referee, Collina, going around the goal area begging the Bayern boys to stand up and finish the game.

'You think of it as having two games: you can do nothing about the 90 minutes that have gone; you've lost that game 1–0. The mindset has to be: this is your return game, and it's only three minutes. You're going to win that game. Manchester United did.'

'You always have to be aware that you might need different types of coaches at different stages of your development,' suggests Judy Murray. 'At the very top, you need somebody within your coaching team who has operated at that level and is comfortable in that environment. If not, it could lead to a loss of confidence and not being comfortable in the area that you are performing in. You need to be absolutely positive that your coach fits in and knows what he or she is doing. There also needs to be a fit of personality. You need to want to be with them and trust them completely, because you have to follow their advice.'

Judy's son Andy famously split with renowned American coach Brad Gilbert in the summer of 2007, a decision that was questioned by many critics. Why would a young, still improving player rid himself of one of the best coaches in the world? When he made the decision Murray said: 'The time has come to move on to the next stage of my career. I am ranked 11 in the world and can now afford to pay my own way, and so I will now hire a team of experts, each to fulfil a specified role in the development of my tennis and fitness.'

'From Andy's point of view,' says Judy, 'there are a number of people whose individual expertise he taps into. A lot is made of the fact that he has a big team, but at most tournaments he will usually only have the physical coach and the travelling coach with him. His technical expert is back in London, fine-tuning the technical side of his game. He will have a video analyst working remotely. He has a physical expert in America. And his agent helps to make things tick, too. They are never all around at the same time. They all have different functions.'

The first step in the path to choosing the right coach is being comfortable with the person and their role. As we said before, the word 'coach' has many meanings. It could be a manager. It could be a mentor. It could be a motivator. It could simply be someone to record your times or stats for you. As long as they are doing the job you need done, as Judy Murray reminds us.

'It's about knowing who you feel you can go to, and who you want to go to. It's about who can give you independent advice that you trust. It needn't always be "a coach". It could be a consultant or an expert who would prefer to be on the sidelines rather than be there on a daily basis.

Or it could be a parent or a former athlete who has been there before. It just needs to be someone whose opinion you trust and respect.'

MENTOR ME

Trust and respect do indeed go a long way, as it did when Scottish teenagers Ruaridh Cunningham and Chris Hutchens put their faith in Chris Ball to help them conquer the downhill mountain-biking world. Ball, himself only 25, had experienced life as a world-class downhiller, travelling the World Cup circuit for several years, before a knee ligament injury put a halt to his career. However, his talent wasn't left to waste away, and Ball was given the charge of 'mentoring' two of Scotland's finest young mountain bikers – Ruaridh, from Melrose, and Oban's Chris Hutchens. Their ultimate goal was success in the junior category at the 2007 Mountain Biking World Championships in Fort William.

'I said I would be supportive for them more than anything, because I never really had a mentor,' explained Ball, a few weeks before the big day at 'Fort Bill', as it is known in extreme sports circles. 'Mountain biking is not yet a big sport in Scotland, so I just try to give them advice on how to progress their career. With Ruaridh and Chris it is important to teach them how to behave on top of and outside of training, and how to be intelligent about their riding. It is very important for them to have role models: that will help Scotland produce more world champions.

'I've passed on all the stuff I do as a rider myself. For example, I took them to see a sports psychologist, who will help us develop a coping strategy to deal with the type of pressure that will come at the World Championships. There will be a huge amount of people watching these guys. The sport is predominantly psychological at this stage, so to know that they've got 100 per cent backing is really important. I know that when I was racing I was always worried about how to get to a race and how I could afford to get there. They don't have to worry about that, it's more relaxed. They can just ride their bike and watch the band after the race!'

Ruaridh Cunningham and Chris Hutchens are both deeply grateful for the help Chris Ball has given them.

'He's a legend,' says Hutchens. 'He has helped us a lot this year and he has taken off the pressure of organising the trips, so we can concentrate more on preparation, which gives us a big advantage over the other riders.'

Cunningham backs him up. 'I was a bit of a pie and needed to get fitter for my last year as a junior and to get my chance at Fort William. So he told me to get my act together to make sure I have a good shot at the title. He will call me up every week and tell me what I need to do, and I'll listen to him.

'He set out a programme for me with full explanations of what to do every day. I'll maybe do weights one day and then a turbo session or sprints the next, and maybe cross-country at the weekend. Every day I will have something planned, whether it is rest or otherwise. You could pretty much report to Chris with anything and he will send you in the right direction and keep you right.'

He kept them right all right. In September 2007, Ruaridh blasted the field out of the water to become the world junior downhill mountain bike champion, while Chris wasn't far behind, finishing in ninth place.

MR MOTIVATOR

While Chris Ball acts as a mentor for Cunningham and Hutchens, other individuals may desire a different kind of coaching assistance. Perhaps you are experienced and disciplined enough to do without a 'role model'. Perhaps that's the problem. You've seen it all. You know the ropes, but there's no incentive to climb them. You are short of inspiration to actually get out there and put your expertise into action. You need motivation. You need Frank Dick.

Yes, if there is a man in Scotland who knows how to manage and motivate, it is Dr Frank Dick. Edinburgh born and raised, this coaching guru has worked, and won, with some of the greatest sportsmen and women to have walked the earth, including Wimbledon legend Boris Becker and iconic British athletes Daley Thompson and Denise Lewis.

MAKING THE RELATIONSHIP WORK

Competitive swimming is tough and intense. It is human body against human body in tests of speed and endurance. And records are broken at almost every major international meet. Why has swimming advanced so rapidly? While there are discussions about the water-resistant qualities of new swimsuits, it is elite coaching that has made the significant difference.

There is no substitute for pure physical conditioning in swimming – and that can become arduous and even tedious. Thankfully, there are guys such as Fred Vergnoux around to ensure that there is a varied and interesting training regime.

Fred was the coach to the City of Edinburgh team from 2004 to 2008 working with Kirsty Balfour, Gregor Tait and Kris Gilchrist. Appointed to the UK's Swimming Leadership Group, which played a massive part in guiding the Olympic squad (including ten Scots in a team of 35) through Beijing in 2008, he is one of the best swimming coaches in Europe.

Vergnoux explains how his training methods inspire his athletes.

'We do several training camps a year abroad, so that we can have more pool time. Mostly we use an outside pool, because competitions take place outside, too. Plus, the breezier conditions can be a bit more challenging and for the swimmers it is a nice oxygen boost to the system.

His scope to rouse and motivate doesn't stop with international sports stars, though. Frank has also worked with many big names in the business world (including Shell, BT and Barclays), giving inspirational speeches to ensure they get out of their staff what he got out of his athletes – performance and results.

Winning, for Frank Dick, is about committing every day to being better than the day before, whether that is in sport, business, education or whatever. You have to be prepared for winning. If you are someone who is just happy to drift along, not pushing yourself to achieve your best, wallowing in mediocrity, you are probably wasting your time reading this book. Frank says you need to be ready to face the challenge.

'Are you going to stand on the edge and step out into that great void? Because not a lot of people will do that. That's why you see athletes choking out there, why you see people out there on the rugby field or the athletics track, thinking, "I've done all the work, it

'Having fun while team-building is important. My team swim 75km a week — about 25 hours in the pool — and do 10–12 hours in the gym. It's a very demanding regime. I try to think of them as athletes first, rather than simply swimmers, so I am keen to have them climbing, mountain biking, kayaking, even hiking. We also do a lot of running — three times every week. I test them on the track as well. I want them trained as proper athletes and to be good at everything.'

Chris Martin, high-performance swimming coach for the Scottish Institute of Sport, has coached some of the world's greatest swimmers, including 1992 Barcelona Olympic Games gold medallist Nelson Diebel. At the Institute in Stirling, Chris oversees a programme that ensures each individual is getting the most out of his or her ability, including the other coaches.

'My big thing all along wasn't just about making the athletes better, it was about improving the athlete-to-coach relationship, so that when the coach gets another swimmer, he or she will be further along than when they got the first one,' explains Martin. 'This gives Scotland a chance to keep improving as a nation. We need every single person, man, woman and child, pulling in the right direction every chance they get.

'I look at athletes in terms of plugging them into what their need is. The coach needs to learn more about their athletes and listen to what they can tell us, learn from them, too, and in this way, gaining a greater understanding of the process of development generally so that this can then be applied to the next athlete.'

should be happening for me now." But it doesn't just happen: you've got to make it happen, and all the training, all the hard work is not something you can just fall asleep on. That's just a foundation.'

Frank uses the metaphor of a highway to describe how, if you want to be successful, everything needs to be functioning correctly. Being a high-performance athlete means you must be a high-performance person. You must be committed to improvement and excellence.

'Your whole life is not like a one-lane carriageway, it's like a three-lane motorway. There's the fast lane: that's your career, or your sport; the middle lane: that's how you relate to the world, your family, society and community. And there's the inside lane – that's you personally. The fact of the matter is that if any one of these lanes is not fully functional, the other two lanes close down, or at least slow down. As a consequence, when you are preparing, developing, you must have targets in all three lanes to grow.'

When we think of winning, we think of Olympic medallists and world champions. Ultimately, however, only one man and one woman will lift the Wimbledon trophy each summer, and only one team can win the World Cup every four years. In the history of time, fewer than 3,000 people have successfully scaled Mount Everest.

But anyone can win by doing as Frank says: being better than the day before, and keeping each lane of your highway in check. Just because it is more achievable doesn't mean it is easy. Climbing your own personal Everest every day is a task that requires a lot more than goodwill. There are three key criteria that he would ask of you if you were to seek his assistance in making it to the top. Read them, and think about each one individually before you move to the next.

Do you want to win?

Do you believe you can win?

Will you persist until you do?

Still with us? Good, because the simple truth is that if you can't answer 'Yes' to these three questions, Frank won't help you. No, that's not right. It's not that he won't help you, it's that he can't. He can't help someone who can't help themselves. And in order to do that, you must strive to be at your very best, all the time.

This is how Frank Dick motivates people. He asks them to challenge themselves, to fight tooth and nail to achieve their goals. He doesn't pull any punches. Life is tough, and winning is tough. So are you motivated? Do you want it? Do you believe you can do it? Will you persist until you do?

'People can get very complicated about motivation,' adds Frank. 'But these three areas are what determine whether you're going to get there or not. The wanting is just the basic desire, that drive to get there. If you don't want to do it in the first place, why the hell are we doing it? That drive's got to be yours. You go into the arena to win, not to be second, not to say, "I'll do just enough."

'There's an acronym that I use in these situations: ODD – Own, Decide and Do. Take ownership of the moment, make a decision and do something about it. You don't know which moment in the game it will turn for you. You don't know that. So you have to visit every moment with excellence. You can't let a moment go by and think "I'll make up for this in two minutes' time." You don't do that; you have to fight for every moment.'

SO WHAT IS A COACH?

In this chapter we have looked at the ways you can take advantage of a coach, and use their knowledge and experience to get the best out of yourself. While we don't believe that there is any single, definitive explanation of what a coach 'does', we decided to ask two top coaches to find out what they think.

Acclaimed athletics coach Tommy Boyle, who took Scottish racers Tom McKean and Yvonne Murray to the pinnacle of world-class distance running in the late 1980s and early 1990s, has a theory on what the role of a coach is: he sees coaching as a blend of two polar opposites.

'Coaching is a mix of art and science. The science is the effective use of proven exercise physiology, in planning the loading, volume intensity and recovery of training in order to maximise the effect whilst minimising the risk of breakdown and injury. The art is the ability to combine the science with practical coaching experience gained over many years to produce consistent results. Both are very important. The skill is in blending them together, and all great coaches can do that.

'Most great coaches have an abundance of common sense. At the same time, they are passionate. That's what my PE teachers at Dalziel High School were like. I don't go in for technical mumbo jumbo. I've seen consultants deliver lectures out of a book, and that's a problem. It's all theoretical. My teachers were inspirational coaching leaders. They inspired me to learn how to motivate.'

In a similar vein, Rangers FC manager Walter Smith says: 'The role of a coach is to form a situation where you can make your team as successful as they possibly can be. And, as they say, success comes in different forms. It might be avoiding relegation, maybe winning the cup, whatever. If you're making a team as successful as they possibly can be, then you are shown to be successful as a manager.

The subject of this statement might equally be an individual athlete; in a nutshell, Smith is explaining the importance of having a coach on board. He himself enjoyed a relatively successful career as a player with Dundee United, but it was when he hung up his boots and became the gaffer that he really came into his own, in club and international football management. His victory against France at Hampden in October 2006 when he was manager of Scotland will never be forgotten. Smith has coached some of the best footballers in the world, and taken a team to the UEFA Cup final. But he has some encouraging advice for you, too.

'I would say to any young person, that if they felt that they had an aptitude for any sport, it's important for them to give their all to that sport, accept disappointments and fight to make themselves as good as they possibly can be. I think if they can do that, then they'll find they will get a great deal of enjoyment out of it. Without a doubt, being involved in a sport will make them a better person.'

THE RIGHT PEOPLE CAN HELP YOU WIN . . .

- Coaching: a coach's job is to make you as successful as you can be.
- Managing: a good manager will guide you and help you with things you find too difficult to do on your own.
- Mentoring: it is worthwhile finding someone who has already done what you want to do. Wise advice gained from experience is a valuable commodity.
- Motivating: we all need a little extra push sometimes, whether it's to work harder, to pick ourselves up after disappointment or to remind us what we're working towards.

THE EXPERTS' OPINION:

MIKE WHITTINGHAM
EXECUTIVE DIRECTOR

Mike has coached and worked with many elite performers both within the UK and worldwide, and has worked at six Olympic Games.

'Winners often have an "obsessive" quality about them, and this strength can be their downfall. Often they "push" too hard and can end up injured or ill. They need to be guided and advised to be smart and make the right choices. This is where the coach/athlete relationship fits in. It can be incredibly powerful and the ultimate differentiator.'

DAVE CLARK
HEAD STRENGTH AND CONDITIONING COACH

Dave is responsible for managing the delivery of strength and conditioning for the Institute. He designs and establishes support programmes for the Institute's core sport programmes and individual athletes, and manages the Institute's strength and conditioning network throughout Scotland.

'A trait that is extremely important for a champion is working on your weaknesses. If you are extremely talented, you can probably get by with less commitment and drive, but if you are slightly less talented, you will probably compensate for that by being extremely dedicated and focused on the process. Top athletes have a clear understanding and commitment to addressing the things that are in deficit.

'I think it is wrong trying to predict if a 14 year old is going to be a champion. It is like predicting a marathon time based on a 5k time. You should just be dealing with them as 14 year olds, not getting ten of them and seeing who will be the Olympic champion.

'You still get senior athletes who are petulant and blame others. And if you expend too much energy trying to apportion blame, trying to find reasons, then you haven't got it yet. I would suspect Steve Redgrave doesn't blame a soul. A winning athlete takes responsibility.'

SCOTLAND'S OLYMPIC GOLD-MEDAL WINNERS

1900 – PARIS
Lorne Currie Yachting (Open class)
Lorne Currie Yachting (Half to 1 tonne class)

1908 – LONDON
Arthur J. Robertson Athletics – 3 mile team race
Wyndam Halswelle Athletics – 400m
Angus Gillan Rowing – Coxless fours
George Cornet Swimming – Water polo
Royal Clyde YC Sailing – 12 metres class

1912 – STOCKHOLM
Henry Macintosh Athletics – 4x100m relay
Philip Fleming Rowing – Eights
Angus Gillan Rowing – Eights
William Kinnear Rowing – Single sculls
Robert Murray Shooting – Small bore rifle team (Over 50m)
George Cornet Swimming – Water polo
Isabella Moore Swimming – 4x100m freestyle relay

1920 – ANTWERP
Robert Lindsay Athletics – 4x400m relay
John Sewell Tug of War – Team
William Peacock Swimming – Water polo

1924 – PARIS
Eric Liddell Athletics – 400m
James McNabb Rowing – Coxless fours
Scottish Team Curling Men

1952 – HELSINKI
Douglas Stewart Equestrian – Show jumping team

1956 – MELBOURNE
Dick McTaggart Boxing – Lightweight

1968 – MEXICO CITY
Rodney Pattison Sailing – Flying Dutchman

1972 – MUNICH
Rodney Pattison Sailing – Flying Dutchman

1976 – MONTREAL
David Wilkie Swimming – 200m breaststroke

1980 – MOSCOW
Allan Wells Athletics – 100m

1984 – LOS ANGELES
Richard Budgett Rowing – Coxed fours

1988 – SEOUL
Veryan Pappin Hockey – Team
Michael McIntyre Sailing – International star class

2000 – SYDNEY
Andrew Lindsay Rowing – Men's eight
Shirley Robertson Sailing – Europe class
Stephanie Cook Modern pentathlon

2004 – ATHENS
Shirley Robertson Sailing – Yngling class
Chris Hoy Cycling – 1km time trial

9

WINNING – ON YOUR TERMS

YOU'VE MADE IT THIS FAR? GOOD WORK. BUT keep going. Have you heard the saying 'all roads lead to Rome'? Well, in this case, all roads lead to winning. It doesn't matter how you choose to digest this book, the outcome should be the same. We want to inspire you to want to win.

In the first three chapters, we went through a selection of the traits that top winners display in their quest for glory – like motivation, determination and belief – while reminding you that those qualities are useless unless you are prepared to put in the time and effort on the training ground. In Chapter 4, we told you how the best athletes in the world rely on deep mental strength as much as physical ability to defeat their opponents, while in Chapter 6 we saw how creating a 'winning culture' is absolutely fundamental to allow such a mindset to flourish. Chapter 5 talks about the team ethos, but a team, or individual, won't function to its full potential without a coach or manager, as we discussed in Chapter 8. And none of this will work unless you can, first and foremost, respect yourself and look after your body, as we mentioned in Chapter 7.

So now, with two chapters to go, this is where we bring it all together. It's time to get down to the nitty-gritty: winning. What is winning? Who are the winners we should aspire to emulate? And, most importantly, can you be a winner? We certainly hope so. Otherwise, you may want a refund!

NEVER, EVER QUIT

In 2000, during a mountain stage of the Tour de France, Lance Armstrong had built up what was assumed to be an unassailable lead of seven and a half minutes by the time he came to a mountain called Joux-Plane. He had been locked in a bitter feud all week with his late, great rival, Marco Pantani over a misunderstanding at an earlier stage of the race. And though Armstrong led the Tour comfortably and could afford to lose the race, Pantani took off ahead of him, goading him to follow. Armstrong, never willing to refuse a challenge, took the bait and chased after the Italian. But so engrossed was he in not letting Pantani win, he made the most elementary of endurance-cycling errors.

'We were riding strong, and I felt good on the bike. So good, that I passed my last chance to eat, and spun through a feed zone without a second thought. It was a feeble mistake, an unthinkable one for a professional, but I made it. We [his team] were so focused on tactics and on Pantani that I forgot to do the simplest thing. It never occurred to me what the consequences of not eating could be,' he says in his memoir, *Every Second Counts*.

Cyclists burn up so much energy in a mountain ascent that not to refuel is sporting suicide. Before long, Armstrong was running on empty, and suffering all the side effects that come with it: hallucinations, extreme fatigue and chills. He even came close to mental breakdown. He could barely see, speak or move. Delirious, he found it within himself to finish the race. That was all he needed to do to stay in the fight. He crossed the finish line at a snail's pace. He should have blacked out. The sensible option would have been for him to have given up ten kilometres before the line and received some urgent medical attention. But not Lance Armstrong.

'I don't know exactly what kept me on the bike, riding, in that state. What makes a guy ride until he's out of his head? I guess, because he can. On some level, the cancer still played a part: the illness nearly killed me, and when I returned to cycling, I knew what I'd been through was more difficult than any race. I could always draw from that knowledge, and it felt like power. I was never really empty. I had gone through all that, just to quit? No. Uh-uh.'

When we decided to entitle this book *Be a Winner*, our objective was not to guarantee you an Olympic gold medal. Our definition of a winner is much more meaningful than shiny coins with a ribbon attached; it is very similar to the magical, motivational words of Dr

Frank Dick in Chapter 8 – being better each day than you were the last. Winning, to us, means getting the best from yourself and for yourself, all the time. John Wooden, the great American basketball coach, says, 'Earn the respect of everyone, especially yourself.' That's not a bad mantra to go by.

Some of you reading this may be elite athletes, so winning may indeed mean standing on the podium at London 2012 or Glasgow 2014. That is the minimum you expect. And if so, we'll be there to cheer you on, that's a promise. For the rest of you, however, winning may mean pushing yourself to make the top team of your local club – be that hockey, athletics, basketball, badminton or whatever. It could mean getting the job you always wanted, passing your exams, learning to drive or starting a course. It doesn't matter what it is; what does matter is that *you* are striving to win for *you*. That's what winning is all about. If you've got potential, go and fulfil it, otherwise you will live to regret it later on in your life.

IT'S NOT ABOUT THE MEDALS

Here's an example of someone who doesn't have an Olympic gold, but is undoubtedly one of the greatest winners that Scotland has ever produced; a woman who dragged herself above those trying to pull her down *to do what she wanted to do*, achieving worldwide glory and recognition in the process. Because that's what winning is all about: doing what you want to do, and doing it well.

OK, when we said she doesn't have an Olympic gold, that might have led you astray a little, because, Olympic champion or not, Liz McColgan is the greatest female runner to have represented Scotland, and is the proud owner of an Olympic silver medal (Seoul 1988) for the 10,000m, and of a World Championship gold, when she trail-blazed her way to a win in Tokyo in 1991. But just like us, Liz McColgan doesn't see the medals as true symbols of what she has achieved with her life. Her hopes and dreams run much deeper than melted and moulded metal.

'I've never been bothered about people that I've beaten, and to be honest, I couldn't tell you where I won the medals, or what time I won the medals in, because it's not of interest to me, not even the big races [like the Olympics and World Championships]. That wasn't what my running was about. My running has always been to see how fast I could go and to be the best that I could be,' says McColgan.

Medals and trophies only mean so much, as Liz explains. Yes, medals are a tangible representation of what you can achieve. Hung in pride of place on the wall or draped round your neck, they are a reminder of a glorious day. But they will only be of significance to the rest of the world for a short while, until someone else comes along to displace you.

Like job titles or exam grades, medals, shields, plaques, cups and bowls are only the visible evidence of the effort you have made in a process that has taken weeks, months or even years. To the individual or team, the honour lies in the work and commitment put in to achieve that prize, title or grade. True winning is the sense of wellbeing that can only come from knowing that you have completed a job, and completed it with pride. Take Liz's advice. Make doing what you want, and doing it well, your priority.

'My advice to anybody is, if you want to do it, go for it. Don't limit your dreams. It doesn't matter what anyone else thinks of you. If you are capable of doing it, then do it.'

HOW LIZ MCCOLGAN BECAME A NATIONAL HERO AND A REAL SCOTTISH WINNER

Liz McColgan wasn't a gifted youngster. She says so herself all the time. She wasn't fast-tracked to the top the way many elite stars are today. She didn't crave the limelight. Her reasons for running were very personal.

'The reason I liked running isn't because I was good at it, I always maintain I was never very talented. I liked running because of what it gave to me. There was an awful lot going on around me when I started, and the running meant I could get away from that and be on my own. And in some weird, sadistic way, the more I hurt, the better I liked it. It was like I could control what I was doing, and nobody could control me. I've always been able to push myself and be very disciplined to get the best out of myself, and I think that running was a great way for me to use those attributes.'

Liz didn't have it easy. Just because she had a passion for running didn't mean everyone else supported her. She needed grit, desire and zeal every step of the way to world glory. This is why she remembers the hard times and the tough stuff, rather than having the medals draped around her neck.

'There were a lot of setbacks. I didn't have a lot of support. Wherever I went, people were always saying, "You'll never do this, you'll never do that." It was very difficult. I found that just because of where I came from, the way I was brought up, doors were closed to me, and it was very hard to break that down. All through my career, I just had to take charge of things for me, for myself, and just keep at it. I really did put an awful lot of work into what I did.'

ROGER'S MOST POWERFUL WEAPON

Roger Federer is one of the most accomplished athletes competing in the world today. Year after year he continues to dominate men's tennis and win at the highest level. But how does he do it? How does he keep on winning, all the time?

According to Roger, who spoke to *Be a Winner* at the World Sports Awards in St Petersburg in 2008, it all starts with what goes on upstairs in the head.

'It's ironic. My mental game used to be my most negative aspect, but now the most powerful weapon in my game is my mental ability to rise to the occasion.

'I think there is also a need for physical ability and talent, but that's not enough, you have to work on it and really have to want it. That's the way you become a champion; it's not enough to rely on your talent.

'I was smart enough and lucky enough to realise that I didn't want to become just a good player, but the best. And that for me was the key to working hard, every day, and enjoying it. I am playing tennis because I love this sport, not for fame, or money.

'I'm very motivated. I have a great hunger to do more and achieve more. I'm still only 26. The reason I went away from tennis for two weeks after losing the Australian Open was because it was always my plan, winning or losing, to reflect. To see what I've done and revise my goals.'

Growing up on the outskirts of Dundee, Liz was laughed at. People mocked her for daring to be different. Being a runner was odd enough, but being a female one was even stranger.

'I would get bullied. A gang of boys would shout at me, call me a weirdo or say, "What are you running for, what are you doing that for?" I went through an awful lot of problems at school because I was different and didn't hang out drinking Babycham and lager with friends. That was difficult, because you are growing up feeling alienated, just because you are doing something that you want to do. You don't really know why you are doing it, but you are.'

As you can see, Liz was up against it in her quest to be the best. She didn't have much help. She didn't even have a TV in her house, and so she didn't have the chance to watch international stars and be inspired by them, as so many youngsters are today. But she persevered, and she did have an I AM moment, an epiphany that gave her the kick in the right direction to step up her training and take on the world.

'When I was 15, I was captain of all the school teams – netball, hockey and volleyball – and my coach said to me, "You're going to have to stop all this, you need to step up your running." At the time, I was only running the 800m and 1,500m, but he said that I was actually a 10,000m runner. That blew me away, because women could only run 3,000m back then, they weren't allowed to run the 10,000m and I was like, "What are you on?! That's six miles, women aren't allowed to do that!" He said, "I'm telling you now, in the next few years the 10,000m will be in for the women and you're going to win at it."

'It shows that he saw something in me, something that I didn't see in me. He was the only person who ever gave me anything positive back about my running, and when he said that I started to think, "Maybe I can do something", and that's when I started to think I could go and win the UK Championships or even a Commonwealth Games. It hadn't been a thought before. And if he hadn't said that or seen something in me, it might never have happened.'

That day started the ball rolling for what, four years later, would become the most significant day of Liz Lynch's (her maiden name) young life, and remains so today, more than 20 years later. With the help of her coach, Harry Bennett, she gradually built herself up for the 1986 Commonwealth Games in Edinburgh where, sure enough, women were granted the right to race the 10,000m.

'We operated in a club system, and there were British champions amongst us, but Harry took me aside and said that I needed to train with him a few extra days on my own. He took me out of the group and spent time with me. I used to meet him on his lunch hour and do extra sessions. He gave me everything I needed to go on. He was the guy who threw distance-running books at me, getting me to read about training. He understood why he was doing things and what I had to do. So he really educated me.'

Then the hard work started; or at least, the work started. Liz wasn't bothered by a bit of elbow grease. Hard work was good work in her mind.

'You think it's hard at the time, but it's the sense of achievement after that gives you the buzz, knowing you just ran ten miles at 4.45 minutes per mile. There aren't a lot of people in the world who can do that. I always used to convince myself that people were training harder than me and that I had to get up and do it. That's the way I motivated myself all the time.'

And the training paid off. On a typically rainy day at Meadowbank Stadium in July 1986, 19-year-old Liz Lynch introduced herself to the world of international athletics with a bang, defeating her nearest rival, New Zealand's Anne Audain, by 12 seconds in the 10,000m. It was a day that will never leave her. It was the culmination of all her effort and desire that makes the win so special for Liz. The magnitude of the event itself was of little consequence.

'The greatest experience I ever had all throughout my running career was the Commonwealth Games in 1986, even though it was a lower level competition. Never since have I experienced the emotions of winning on that day. Nothing comes near to it.

'When I was called out to receive my medal, I could hear everyone shouting my name and saw that the whole place was packed with people. It was unbelievable, the best moment in my life. It could actually be seen as one of the worst things that happened to me, because nothing else ever lived up to it! Even when I was a world champion, it didn't feel the same. And to have the home crowd there makes such a difference.'

This was what winning for Liz felt like when all the effort and sacrifice paid off. And we might see a similar moment unfolding with some Scottish athletes when the Commonwealth Games come back to Scotland in 2014.

'If anybody wins a gold medal in Glasgow, it would be fantastic. It will be a great experience for all the athletes who take part.'

HIT THE WINNING RUN

The South Africa-born Scotland cricket captain for the 2007–08 season, Ryan Watson, has learned a lot from his sport: how to be competitive, how to think correctly under pressure and, of course, the skills and fitness that can only come from being involved in sporting activity. But most of all, he says, he has learned how to be a leader, both of others and of himself. He is conscious of applying the traits he has learned in sport to his day job.

'Being captain of Scotland, you acquire leadership qualities which can easily be transferred into the workplace. Man-management on the sports field is very similar in business. Those skills are transferable.

'You learn to set yourself personal targets, take everything into consideration: your social life, your working life — and you go out and achieve your personal targets. That's crucial in any sport: you have to set yourself targets. And as long as you can look back and say you have achieved 80 or 90 per cent of what you have set, I think you have been successful, you have won.

'But the biggest thing I have got from sport is mates. I have come to a new country and met a lot of good friends from cricket. If I look back on ten years of cricket in Scotland, that has been the biggest thing for me, the amount of friends I have made.'

AROUND THE WORLD IN 194 DAYS – IT'S ABOUT THE JOURNEY, NOT THE DESTINATION

If you were to take a trip round the world, you wouldn't want to teleport your way from start to finish, would you? You would want to experience all the wonderful sights and sounds in between. Similarly, if you want to be a winner, you wouldn't want to just arrive at your goal without knowing what it took to get there, would you?

When Mark Beaumont, from Fife, was 12 years old, he saw a report in a newspaper about how a local man cycled from John o'Groats to Land's End. That set his mind racing. He wanted to do it too. His mum, ever keen to encourage, but wary of him taking on a 1,000-mile bike-ride without any experience, suggested he should have a practice run first, so instead Mark rode 145 miles from Dundee to Oban, raising £2,000 for charity in the process. Cycling was to play a very significant role in Mark's life from that moment onwards. Having conquered his first major challenge, he was hungry for more. Eventually he did the End To End route in Great Britain that he had so craved as a pre-teen, and even took on the Arctic Circle a few years later. Then, in 2007, aged 25, Mark took on the biggie: to circumnavigate the whole world by bike, raise thousands for charity and break the world record in the process.

'I knew when I left university that I wanted to take on one big adventure, and basically I couldn't think of a bigger one,' said Beaumont, just a few weeks after he returned from his adventure in early 2008. 'I can't remember the exact moment when it occurred to me. I think people have these fleeting thoughts all the time, but they are so small and insignificant they don't do anything about it. I think that quite often people wait for lightning to strike, but the world doesn't work like that. You have thoughts all the time and it's a case of developing them. It is very hard to define the first point of realisation for any dream. It is just important to realise that during the course of every day you will have ideas, and it's about grabbing hold of them and making something of them.'

Much like Liz McColgan, Mark dared to do. He was just a normal guy. In fact, he still is. He's not a professional sportsman, just a young man with amazing self-belief and determination. When everyone else was pottering around about him, he was taking action on the grandest scale. Like Liz, he wasn't doing it for the glory or the accolades.

Mark is a journey man first and foremost, not a destination man. And his journey took him from Paris, down to Istanbul, through Asia, stopping in Calcutta, Bangkok and Singapore, across central Australia and to the south tip of New Zealand, from west coast to east coast USA, then back to Paris via Lisbon.

'If you just did it for the world record, it would be a pretty empty cause. That wouldn't motivate me. You have to be in it for the journey. That's the thing that's quite often missing with ambition of any sort. People have a lot of ideas, but they don't realise the work that has to be put in, all they want to do is get to the final destination.

'You have to enjoy the journey and what you are doing. That's something that's slightly missed in our society. People go into careers to get the lifestyle they want, as opposed to wanting to do the job: they see where they want to be but sometimes hate the journey which gets them to that place. You have to be in it for the journey.'

Mark travelled 18,000 miles, at a rate of 100 miles per day, over a period of 194 days. That means in nearly seven months, he only took 14 days off. Aside from the sheer physical strain of riding a bike for ten hours a day, he was battered by monsoon rains, scorched by desert sun, mugged, knocked off his bike by a donkey and afflicted by food poisoning. But he kept his cool the whole way, and made it back to his starting point in Paris. How did he do it?

'I never ever thought about it as an 18,000-mile race. Everyone saw it in macro terms, whereas I saw it in micro terms, and I split the race into seven legs. I had done the route setting and preparations myself, so I knew every detail of what I was about to do. Then it was simply a case of getting on the road, forgetting about tomorrow, forgetting about yesterday and getting through each moment. When it got tough, it was about shortening your targets; when it was easier, you could allow yourself a longer target.'

Mark's body underwent massive stress while riding. As well as muscle strain, there were what he calls 'conditioning sores' – pains and wounds that develop purely from sitting on a saddle for hours and hours, such as back pain from being crouched over, tension headaches, blisters and chafing.

'I would have really bad headaches or sores, but when you have a flow going, you can think through them, your mental focus is above all the physical aches and pains. The one time I really hit the wall was in the Australian outback. The roads were better and things were easier than they had been through Asia, but for some reason I started losing it in terms of my mental focus. I started thinking about the big picture, how far I had to go.

'The mind is not particularly good at dealing with huge targets and huge numbers, but what the human mind is fantastic at doing is routine. It doesn't matter how hard that routine is, as long as you have structure to your day and you absolutely focus on the next small target.'

On top of all this, there is the obvious fact that he was absolutely knackered.

'I was exhausted all the way around. It is very hard to relate to normal tiredness. If you run a marathon, you will be tired, but you have a good night's sleep afterwards. If you cycle 100 miles every single day, it becomes a deep fatigue, mentally and physically, which is very hard to describe if you haven't been there. It's a long time to be kept going. You get to a stage where you are really aware of living off your last meal and your last sleep. At a couple of stages transferring from continent to continent overnight, I lost a night's sleep. That hit me for a week afterwards, because I was so in tune with what I was living off.'

So next time you're having a tough day, think about what Mark went through. He persevered with sheer doggedness and determination. He wasn't a quitter, because winners never quit, and quitters never win. And the feeling of winning is too good to miss out on.

'Those last few miles, I had lots of thoughts going through my head. After six and a half months of that routine, all those demands mentally and physically, it was about to be over; I was about to see my family and friends again, and at that point that was all that mattered. It wasn't about the world record, it was about finishing and being back, after such a long time on my own. I was pretty emotional those last couple of miles. There was an incredible sense of climax. It was incredible, that natural sense of finale. I have never experienced anything like it, and it felt wonderful. So different from what I imagined. It's not really jumping up and down with excitement, it is a deep sense of satisfaction.

'You can get that essential satisfaction from pushing whatever your comfort levels are. You can be at the top level, but if you don't achieve as well as you think you can, even if you do actually win, then you will get less satisfaction than someone with a regular 9–5 job, going out to do a 5k and beating their personal best. It's not as if these people at the top of their game have a greater level of satisfaction than anyone else who is achieving by pushing their own comfort zones.'

SOME MORE SCOTTISH WINNERS

Mark and Liz are just two examples of what aspiring to get the best from yourself and for yourself can achieve. They were humble people from modest backgrounds who went out and did something amazing. But there is no secret to what they have done. It's written down in plain English on these pages. And there are hundreds and thousands and maybe even millions more winners, walking past you every day.

Next time you see an old man walk by you in the street, or sitting beside you on the bus, think about what he has done with his life. Does he look like a man with a deep sense of satisfaction, such as what Liz and Mark talk about? Well, maybe if you are sitting next to Jackie Brown or Bill McFadyen, you will understand what we mean.

On Friday 25 July 1958, red-headed Jackie Brown from Edinburgh won a gold medal in the flyweight contest of the Empire Games (now the Commonwealth Games) in Cardiff, beating Tommy Bache from Liverpool. Jackie was a dandy fighter, lithe and athletic, who danced through his bouts. Although small and compact, he packed a lethal punch which claimed a number of impressive victims.

Describing the final bout, the *Daily Record*'s boxing correspondent, Peter Wilson, said: 'Before the fight was more than half a minute old, Bache was down on the seat of his pants from a vicious right cross to his jaw. Brown, who had met Bache earlier in the season and had floored him four times, obviously had the answer to the southpaw . . . and by the end of the second round Bache was smothered in blood from a nose whose course was distinctly "off true".'

Jackie soon turned professional, winning the British and Empire titles. He fought 145 bouts, including 43 professional fights, 33 wins and nine losses.

'I was never out-pointed in my professional career,' he says.

When Jackie retired from the ring in the late 1960s, he continued to train local football teams. And even today, in his seventies, the 'Phantom Dancer' is still remarkably light on his toes. Rocking and rolling at every opportunity, he worked in Marco's Leisure Centre in Edinburgh, where he taught boxing training – putting youngsters a quarter of his age through their paces right up until its closure in 2008. That's winning all right. Jackie has that sense of satisfaction.

Longevity at the top in sport is something that few achieve. But 70-year-old Willie Wood, the Scottish bowler from Haddington, had a remarkable span: from 1966 until 2002, when he was 64, he won two Commonwealth Games gold and two World Bowls Championships runner-up medals, and became the first Scot to compete in seven Commonwealth Games.

Or maybe take a look around next time you're in a gym in the Dumfries area. You might just bump into 74-year-old Bill McFadyen. And if you do, you'll probably need him to help you back up, because, despite his age, he is one of the strongest men in the world. Bill is the king of the bench press, lifting 172.5kg in September 2007. He is a local celebrity, and ambassador, travelling all over the world, and has been representing his country with distinction for decades.

'I was drawn to weightlifting from a very early age. I was 16 when I joined a gym and started training with weights. I was conscripted into the Army for three years, then when I left I took up powerlifting. I entered the Scottish and British championships. I was doing natural bodybuilding competitions, but realised this was not my scene, so I returned to powerlifting with great success in domestic and international championships.

MONTY ON WINNING

Good old golf. The Scots have always excelled in the sport they invented, from Old and Young Tom Morris pioneering the modern game in the 19th century, to Sandy Lyle and Sam Torrance becoming national heroes in the 1980s, to Paul Lawrie winning the Open in 1999.

Colin Montgomerie is probably Scotland's best-known golfer internationally. He knows a thing or two about winning. The vital linchpin in several Ryder Cup campaigns, he won the European Order of Merit for seven consecutive years, and in 2007 he won the World Cup Trophy for Scotland with compatriot Marc Warren. We had a little Q&A with Monty to get the lowdown on being a winner.

Who or what inspired you as a young man into becoming a top player?

I just wanted to play the sport I love full-time as my profession, and was lucky enough to be successful. I admire lots of golfers — Seve Ballesteros, Nick Faldo, Jack Nicklaus, the greats. But I think I would credit my dad as the single person who most inspired me to go for it. I needed his support to get the opportunity to try my hand at professional golf, and he has always been behind me 100 per cent. Much of the motivation does come from within, though.

What are the key ingredients behind your success?

Competitiveness and thriving under pressure — I am very competitive in everything I do, that is what motivates me. I wouldn't keep playing if I didn't start each tournament believing I can win.

How important is plain old hard work and practice?

There's no substitute for hard work. For instance, my fellow professionals Padraig Harrington, who won the Open at Carnoustie in 2007, and Vijay Singh have a fantastic work ethic and their success is, in part, down to the confidence and consistency that long hours of practice gives them. I practised far harder in the early stages of my career — I am more of a feel golfer than a technical one and as such, if I over-practise, it doesn't feel so natural and I can get stale. If something isn't going well in my game, then I would obviously work hard on it to sort it out. At the end of the day, I am a perfectionist. But, for me, nothing beats the thrill of competition.

Where do intelligence, self-belief and mental attitude come in? At the top level, does the ability to outwit or psych out your opponent count for a lot?

Self-belief and intelligent course management are certainly crucial in golf, but generally we play stroke-play events and they are about playing the course, not an opponent. Even in match play, it doesn't become personal with your opponent, although I do enjoy the one-to-one aspect. It is still very much about playing the course, though — you can take more risks than you do in a stroke-play event.

How would you define the term 'winning mentality'?

That comes into play when you are having an off day, when things don't feel right but you manage to stay mentally tough and grind out a good score. There is no one better at this than the number one golfer, Tiger Woods.

How does the dynamic differ when it comes to team-play?

It's difficult to pinpoint exactly why our team spirit is so strong. But personally, I really enjoy the cut and thrust of match play, it just seems to bring out the best in my game.

Are nutrition, hydration, proper rest and conditioning essential to the 21st-century golfer?

I'm a lot more knowledgeable about nutrition and fitness than I used to be and although I am certainly a long way from being a fitness fanatic, I do go in the gym regularly and when I am playing in hot weather, I am diligent about keeping hydrated.

Is coaching important to you? How much reliance do you place in a coach to get you to the level you want to be?

Coaching is important but I don't think you can rely on anyone other than yourself when you get out on the course. I would certainly advise any amateur to invest in lessons, as it is far easier to learn the right habits than undo the bad ones you form without coaching.

How would you define 'winning'? What makes someone a winner — and can anybody be a winner?

I think a winner is about being the best you can be. If you try your hardest to achieve the most you possibly can and never give up, then you are a winner in my book, and that applies to anything you set your mind to.

SCOTLAND'S GOLDEN RECORD AT
THE COMMONWEALTH GAMES

Scotland's athletes have had a chequered history when it comes to the Commonwealth Games. In the first seven British Empire Games — which became the British Empire and Commonwealth Games in 1950, before taking on the tag we know today in 1978 — Scotland netted 37 gold medals, with our boxers winning nine of this tally, and diver Peter Heatly winning three. And while the nation had a poor record on the athletics track, we produced two marathon golds with Dunky Wright (1930) and Joe McGhee (1954).

In 1966, Scotland managed only a single gold medal at the Games in Jamaica with the great marathon master, Jim Alder, winning the event in two hours and 22 minutes. He also took a bronze in the six-mile run. By comparison, England won 33, Australia 23 and Canada 14 gold medals. The Scots came a depressing 13th in the medal table, behind Wales, Malaysia and Nigeria. Even the Isle of Man won a single gold.

With Edinburgh hosting the Games in 1970, a dramatic improvement was needed. It turned out to be an exhilarating showcase: Scotland put on its best bib and tucker and delivered a brilliant performance, coming fourth in the medals table with six golds. Among the gold stars were the two Rosemarys — Payne and Stirling — the two Stewarts — Ian and Lachie — boxer Tom Imrie and fencer Sandy Leckie.

In 1974, Scotland managed only three golds, with David Wilkie delivering two in the

'An old injury prevented me from participating in two of the three required [powerlifting] lifts. Luckily the Masters [40s and over] Bench Press Championships were born and held in Killeen, Texas where I won my first gold in this new event. In the same year I also picked up gold in the European Championships. Since then till the present day I have continued to bring home gold, become champion of champions, the world champion at Masters 3 [over 60s] category and set two world records.'

Bill's a winner. Every day he pushes himself to the limit. And he isn't planning on stopping. He is, literally, raising the bar all the time. And he doesn't want to stop. 'If there isn't a way, I'll have to find a way,' says Bill, in his quest to bench ever-heavier weights.

And for every older winner, there is a new one rising through the ranks, ready to do Scotland proud. Consider the teenage golfers Sally Watson and Carly Booth. Both are phenomenally gifted players of swimming pool. In 1978, in Edmonton, it was three more again, with Allan Wells taking a single and then a relay gold, and small-bore rifle shooter Alister Allan — Scotland's greatest-ever Commonwealth Games competitor with ten medals — taking the third gold.

In Brisbane, in 1982, Scotland had one of its most successful Commonwealth Games, with Meg Ritchie winning the discus and Allan Wells taking a double in the 100m and 200m. However, the home support in Edinburgh four years later, in 1986, had little to cheer about apart from Liz Lynch's (now McColgan) 10,000m victory at Meadowbank, along with bowlers George Adrian and Grant Knox and badminton doubles pair Billy Gilliland and Dan Travers winning gold.

The 1990s started well with five golds in Auckland, New Zealand. Then in 1994, in British Columbia, that tally increased to six, with bowler Richard Corsie and 10,000m runner Yvonne Murray among the stars. In Malaysia, in 1998, Scotland managed only three again, with boxer Alex Arthur and squash player Peter Nicol, who swapped to become an English representative, taking gold alongside bowlers Margaret Letham and Joyce Lindores.

The 2002 Games in Manchester were an outstanding success for the city, but Scotland brought back only six golds. It was in Melbourne, in 2006, that the team achieved the impressive 11 gold rush — led by the swimmers — which bodes well for Delhi 2010 and 2014 in Glasgow.

their sport, but are already showing the intelligence, commitment and application that will see them rise through the rankings to the very top of their game.

Aged 17 and 16 respectively, Watson and Booth represented the Great Britain and Ireland Ladies' team at the Curtis Cup in St Andrews in 2008. They are two of the youngest players to have represented GB and I at this level, Booth being the youngest ever. At 14, Sally jumped the pond to take up a golf scholarship at David Leadbetter's Golf Academy in Florida. Determined to make the best of herself in a game she has played competitively from the age of six, it hasn't taken her long to learn the traits of winning.

'In golf, as in any other sport, there might be someone who has worked harder and is more talented than you. Everyone's potential is different. And, of course, the best player I might possibly become still might not be enough to be the very best. But if you can go out onto a golf course and play to the best of your potential, you might not win the tournament – but your main competition is against yourself and whether you can reach perfection. So it is about playing to the very best of your ability. I believe you're a winner if you can do that,' Sally says.

WINNING WITH THE WORLD'S GREATEST

To conclude this chapter, just in case you're not convinced yet, we asked some of the greatest international sportsmen and women in the world about winning. Because we want to prove to you what winning is really about, what it really means. Here's what they said . . .

TONY HAWK, THE WORLD'S MOST SUCCESSFUL SKATEBOARDER

'Being a winner is doing your absolute best. In my career I was happy if I performed the best that I could, regardless of how I ended up in the standings. Because it really was the best I could do. I can't do any better than that. Even if I won and I didn't perform my best, I didn't feel good about it, because I felt like I was capable of more.'

CAROLINA KLUFT, OLYMPIC AND THREE TIME WORLD CHAMPION HEPTATHLETE

'Winning for me is to win over yourself, to beat yourself all the time and try to improve yourself in every single aspect of your life, mentally and physically. Try to get better all the time and do your best. I don't find my inspiration in thinking that I have to win. It's more about "I have to do my best and I have to have fun". Everyone has to find their own way to motivate themselves. We all have different sources of inspiration. You just have to find your own way.'

SEAN FITZPATRICK, WORLD CUP-WINNING NEW ZEALAND RUGBY PLAYER, 92 CAPS FOR THE ALL BLACKS, CAPTAINING THEM FROM 1992 TO 1997

'Winning is knowing that when you have done something, that you have given it a good shot. You have given yourself every opportunity to win. If you don't win, at least you know. That's how we [the All Blacks] define it.'

ANNIKA SORENSTAM, WORLD NO. I GOLFER 2006, WINNER OF TEN MAJORS

'Determination, focus and dedication – these are the things that have helped keep me at the top for so long. I never give up. I always keep grinding away. Put all these things together and you have what has helped me to sustain such a long and successful career.'

TANNI GREY-THOMSON – WINNER OF 16 PARALYMPIC MEDALS, INCLUDING 11 GOLD, ACROSS FIVE OLYMPIC GAMES (1988, 1992, 1996, 2000, 2004)

'A winner doesn't have to be someone who wins medals. Winning, for me, was being the best I could.'

SCOTLAND'S 11 GOLD MEDALS AT THE 2006 COMMONWEALTH GAMES

Boxing: Kenneth Anderson – light heavyweight division.

Cycling: Chris Hoy, Craig MacLean and Ross Edgar – team sprint.

Bowls: Alex Marshall and Paul Foster – men's doubles.

Shooting: Sheena Sharp and Susan Jackson – women's 50m rifle prone pairs; Sheena Sharp – women's 50m rifle prone individual.

Swimming: David Carry – men's 400m freestyle; David Carry – men's 400m individual medley; Caitlin McClatchey – women's 200m freestyle; Caitlin McClatchey – women's 400m freestyle; Gregor Tait – men's 200m backstroke; Gregor Tait – men's 200m individual medley.

WHY WINNING IS SO IMPORTANT . . .

- You will never forget what you achieve: pictures fade, medals get put in drawers, but the memories and satisfaction will never leave you.
- It's about the journey: we all want to be successful, but the most rewarding part of success is what you did to attain it.
- It doesn't matter who you are or what you do: everyone can be a winner if they try hard enough.
- Be a Winner: the true winner is someone who strives to be better and reach his or her potential every day.

THE EXPERTS' OPINION:

DAVE CROSBEE
HEAD OF PERFORMANCE PLANNING

Dave is in charge of planning and organisation for the various athletes supported by the Institute. He creates programmes for individuals and for specific sports, including hockey, judo, golf and weightlifting. He represented and coached the GB Canoe Slalom Team.

'A champion has a real doggedness about what they do. They just won't give up. For some that is truly intrinsic, which you see in a model athlete like Campbell Walsh or Chris Hoy.

'Top athletes have an appreciation of the process needed to get a result, not just the outcome. The outcome is obviously important, but it doesn't just happen. You have to go through some sort of process to get there, and you have to have some form of appreciation for that. If you understand the process, and you know you have done everything possible to address it, that's where the self-belief comes from.

'Winners are not afraid to confront their weakness. That is perfectly achievable for anyone in any aspect. It comes down to asking yourself what you are good at, what you're not so good at, and addressing the areas you are not good at.

'Talent is not the defining factor. My personal theory is that those with more talent fail in the long term because winning came easier to them. They didn't have that work ethic, that ability to really understand and explore the process of becoming better. They got there really quickly, really easily, and then all of a sudden it got hard. And if you haven't got that ethic embedded in you, you will struggle.'

10

BE A WINNER IN LIFE

THERE IS REALLY NO FINISHING LINE FOR THE winner in sport. It's a mirage. When you do decide to hang up your boots or put away your hockey stick in the cupboard, there is a life waiting for you beyond the sports field. Many of the lessons learned by those months and years of training, practice, taking part and competing can be translated into the way you lead the rest of your life.

If you're fortunate, you might even be able to make a living or a career in sport – and you don't have to be a Scottish football pundit or a former international rugby star to make a decent living. The sports industry remains one of the fastest-growing sectors in the world, employing tens of thousands of people in Scotland alone, from greenkeepers to stadium administrators and sports journalists, through to match-day security, programme sellers and officials.

The winning mentality you have been developing in your sport does carry through into other aspects of your life. Bill Shankly, the Scottish-born manager of Liverpool, said in 1973: 'Some people think football is a matter of life and death. I don't like that attitude. I can assure them it's much more serious than that.' These have become immortal words, but perhaps Lucinda Green, the British Olympic horse-rider, sums up sport better when she says: 'Sport is the University of Life.'

'Being a Winner' prepares you for the trials and the tribulations of modern life. While some people have the privilege of their upbringing and family wealth to get them up the ladder, no one is entitled to anything in this world. But we all have a responsibility to do what we can with the talents we have, and that means trying to deal with our own personal circumstances. There are so many jumps, hoops and hurdles – look, these sporting metaphors are popping up again – and having a sporting mindset does, in general, help you tackle them more easily.

Winning and the prospect of defeat are an ingrained part of our daily lives; how you handle this can define how you are as a human being. We all have to face life and death at some point – and this can appear bleak and bewildering. But, as Scots, we can't blame anyone else for our own situation – it's up to us to find ways of turning the negative into the positive.

Developing that winning attitude throughout your life will help. Even if your one sporting achievement has been to play in the local scratch team that won a Monday-night five-a-side tournament, or finishing the course in a school swimming gala, you will have experienced that sense of pride of being part of the event. Your participation has helped make the event more competitive. And while you might be some distance away from becoming an elite athlete, if your performance has improved by a fraction, then you are en route to becoming a winner. That's the kind of electricity that spurs you on to achieve a personal best. That's the kind of energy that more Scots need to use to ensure physical and indeed mental wellbeing throughout their lives.

This isn't just a selfish pursuit either. There is a common good in being able to share other people's incremental success. While we all loved watching Chris Hoy win the World Championship in Manchester in March 2008, and we relished Scottish success for Great Britain in the Beijing Olympics, we can also enjoy watching other athletes winning in more minor arenas. And when they've done well, we should give them some praise and encouragement, something we've neglected to do for too long in Scotland.

We also need to adopt a much more positive outlook to those around us: if someone wants to be a goal-kicker like Chris Paterson, or a runner like Liz McColgan, and spend extra time on improving their performance, then we need to encourage them, not join the herd and start to mock anyone who wants to be something better – and perhaps a little bit different. It is up to every Scot to be more supportive towards those who want to achieve something positive. If it means climbing every Munro in Scotland, cycling to work every day, walking the Southern Upland Way or running five kilometres in Bellahouston Park, then let's try and support each other's achievements.

Every day, in companies around the globe, business leaders use a host of sporting metaphors to encourage their people to perform better. The modern workplace is full of encouragement for employees and managers to 'Be a Winner' for the business and for your own personal achievement. Just think of Scotland's most successful company, the Royal Bank of Scotland, which is based in Edinburgh at Gogarburn and now plays on a world-class stage. Its slogan is 'Make It Happen' – you see it posted all over Scotland's airport terminals and billboards. The bank uses a range of sporting people from Andy Murray to Sir Jackie Stewart and former Scotland rugby star Andy Nicol to hammer home this message to customers and staff. It also has a gym and swimming facilities for its staff, because it knows the importance of keeping its people fit and active.

If you ask any of Scotland's most successful people, they will all say that being a winner in sport gives them the impetus to be winners in business, too. In a survey of the UK's top chief executives carried out in 2008 by the Isle of Man government, 71 per cent said they honed their leadership and boardroom skills on the sports field.

Sir Tom Hunter, now regarded as Scotland's richest man and a leading philanthropist, made his first fortune by selling sports trainers. He's still a sports fan and remains highly competitive in the business world.

'We need to encourage a greater spirit of "can-do" attitude in our young people, and sport has a central role to play in that. Equally, we need to encourage people to try and, yes, be prepared to fail, but then get back in the ring and win the next time or indeed keep on trying. The American President Franklin Delano Roosevelt once said during the Great Depression in the 1930s: "We have nothing to fear but fear itself." That's correct. For me, one person who embodies all that is brilliant about the Scots and sports is Jamie Andrew. Here's a guy who loses his feet and hands in a terrifying climbing accident in the Alps. So what does he do once he has been rehabilitated? He climbs Mount Kilimanjaro the hard way, then following on from that he completed the Ironman Challenge. In the meantime, what are we all doing?'

The Aberdeen Football Club chairman, Stewart Milne, who is also chairman of the Scottish Premier League, spends most of his time running a major UK business: he established his eponymous business in 1975, and it is now one of Scotland's biggest house-building firms. His winning mentality involves spends three mornings a week in the gym to keep fit and playing golf with his sons – he always aims to win.

'I've always felt that the qualities required for success in business and sport run parallel. Both disciplines require passion and commitment and the need to keep practising in order to learn, improve and be the best you can be.

'I would actively encourage young Scots to take on board those principles. You only get out of life what you put into it. Even in the most difficult of times, keep trying, never give up, always believe. Nothing is beyond you.'

Another successful Scot is Sir Ian Wood, who has built the Wood Group, based in Aberdeen, into one of the world's largest oil service companies, with offices in Venezuela, Argentina, the United States and Russia. Sir Ian has been a competitor all his life and has a winning mentality. Even when he was building up his business, he would return to Aberdeen to play squash at the Mannofield squash club. It has only been recently that he put his racket away.

He sees the importance of determination and a will to succeed.

'Keep trying – don't give up. Learn from failures, have a game plan and play fair,' he says.

He acknowledges the benefits of playing team games in learning to control your temperament. Is being a winner in sport the same as in business? Are there similar traits?

'Not in individual events,' he says. 'This generally depends on significant specialist physical capability and skills. Competitiveness and the will to win applies to both sport and business, but it is possible that the individualism of very successful sportspeople in individual events does not prepare them well for the "working with people" challenges of business,' he adds.

Sir Ian is an advocate of teams.

'In team games, there is significant similarity and analogies. Playing the right role in the team, motivating your fellow players, bringing out the potential in others, analysing the competition and their strengths and weaknesses. Winning at a team sport is based on all of this, as is winning in business.'

There is one piece of advice he would give to young Scots. 'Don't be a spectator. Most of the things that have gone wrong in our world have occurred because good people have stood by and let them happen. Be prepared to become involved, show passion, show initiative and where the challenge presents itself, show leadership.'

And Sir Bill Gammell, who set up Cairn Energy plc, now a major international oil company with its headquarters based in Scotland, played rugby for Scotland, but it was when playing squash that he realised that he needed to adopt a winning mindset. Sir Bill, who has had the vision to create the Winning Scotland Foundation, is determined that all Scots should aim to raise their bar in life.

'At the moment, the bar in Scotland is set too low – we tend to be content with mediocrity. Yet, if Scotland is to succeed in an increasingly competitive sporting and business world, it is vital that our young people aspire to fulfil their potential. As a nation, we've got to have a bigger vision and more self-confidence. Winning is in the mind, and sport is integral to the health of the nation. Winning isn't everything but wanting to win is.

'When I was 15, I reached the final of a tournament and was playing the number one seed, someone I knew was fitter and technically better than me. I was two sets ahead, but I bottled it, and my opponent stormed back to win in the fifth set and secure the trophy. My father was there to watch, and, while he sympathised, he encouraged me to be more determined and have the confidence to follow the challenge through to the very end. I decided at that point that I needed to change my own mindset and believe that I could be a winner.'

There are politicians who have been leading sportspeople. Lord Sebastian Coe became a Tory MP, while Sir Menzies Campbell, the former leader of the Liberal Democrats, was a Scottish sprinter who went to the Olympic Games in Tokyo in 1964. He sees parallels between life and sport.

'The patterns of self-discipline necessary for sporting success are equally powerful in later life. Sport gives a sense of self-worth, personal esteem and self-confidence. There is no direct parallel between sport and politics but both involve "winning" and "losing". Both require application and dedication, but success in politics often depends on luck and circumstances beyond one's control.'

What would he suggest to young people on the path to success?

'Embrace ambition and invite challenges in all you do. Look for the opportunity to prove yourself in every sphere of life.'

Sir Menzies Campbell was a Scottish champion, so what does he recall about his time as an elite athlete running for his country?

'For less than 40 seconds, I was one of the 32 fastest men in the world as I ran in the final of the 4x100m relay. I remember it as clearly as if it were yesterday.'

For most people, sport is fun but it can also mean work – certainly that's the case for the professional athlete; there is also a range of places to work – within clubs and grounds, in sports tourism, marketing and public relations. And for the winners, there is the opportunity of working in the media as a commentator, expert pundit or link person. The best example is Gary Lineker – although racing driver Sir Jackie Stewart is the better Scottish example; he made more money as a television presenter in the United States than he ever did winning three Formula One racing championships.

Susie Elms, the Head of Performance Lifestyle at the Scottish Institute of Sport, has some extra advice for anyone striving to be a winner as much as for winners themselves.

'Our key message is that, as there is so much involvement and pressure in sport, you should try and branch out in other avenues.

You should be looking at other elements of your life that give you a positive distraction away from your sport. Your ability to play at the highest level, your motivation to adhere to training, your organisational skills are all the better for it. My main philosophy is to work towards performance targets, but underlying that is the aim to develop the person as a whole.

'A great achievement for me is seeing a retired athlete return to the job market and go on to be successful. Particularly with developing athletes, it's an important part of our work to widen, not narrow, your athlete's identity. A lot of athletes don't recognise that their sports skills are transferable. When they do, they are often very successful.'

Taking part in your chosen sport does not guarantee that you will have a successful life. But there are plenty of examples of people who have used their winning mindset, built up in the sporting arena, to go on to other highs in life.

In saying this, what qualifies as sport? Perhaps we should have defined this right at the start, but we didn't think that a definition should get in the way.

We all accept that football, cricket, rugby, golf, basketball and athletics are sports, but what about sailing, dog racing, video gaming and scuba diving? The Council of Europe in 2001 defined sport as 'all forms of physical activity which, through casual [informal] or organised participation, aim at expressing or improving physical fitness or mental wellbeing, forming social relationships or obtaining results in competition at all levels'.

Darts, pool and even haggis throwing are types of sports to be enjoyed. And, according to our definition, sport does not have to be competitive as long as it offers a personal challenge.

In all then, how do sport and life actually fit together? That's another book – and one for the philosophers. But we can end with Simon Barnes, the chief sportswriter for *The Times* newspaper, who doesn't claim to have an in-depth knowledge or area of expertise in sport. He just tells the stories: the great dramas, the heartbreak and the glory.

In his book *The Meaning of Sport*, he writes honestly about sport, what it does to us, what it does for us. He concludes: 'Sport is everything:

sport is nothing. Sport is important: sport is trivial. Sport is packed with meaning: sport means nothing . . . Sport is simple: sport is complex. Sport is beautiful: sport is irredeemably ugly. Sport is only about winning: sport is mainly about losing.'

He also says something that in many ways sums up the central theme of *Be a Winner*: 'Look for your strengths: you will find them in the same place as your weaknesses.'

For Barnes, this is an elementary truth about life – and it seems to fit for sport, too. Enjoy your sport – and enjoy your life. Believe that you can be a winner – and you will be.

BE A WINNER IN LIFE . . .

- Try your hand at everything: give yourself as many opportunities as possible by trying new things. You never know what you might excel at.

- Lessons from sport can be taken into all walks of life: career, business, politics, education, health and family. You only have one life – make the most of it.

- Prove and improve: never stop wanting to win. Improve yourself, prove yourself and then go back and improve yourself again.

- Winning is in the mind: if you believe you can do it, then, eventually, you will.

ACKNOWLEDGEMENTS

WE HAVE COVERED A WIDE RANGE OF SPORTS and individuals in *Be a Winner*, but if we have left anybody out, or overlooked their achievements, then we hope we haven't hurt their feelings. Unfortunately, we have been limited by the number of pages on which to write about Scotland's winners. Maybe we will do an encyclopaedia next time.

In *Be a Winner*, we talk at length about the fact that in order to succeed, you must put in the effort. And it is the efforts of many, not just us, the authors, that have allowed this book to be in your hands today.

Foremost, we must say a massive thank you, and offer congratulations, to all the sportsmen and women that have inspired us to write this book. And that goes not just for the athletes and coaches but to all the other people behind the scenes, supporting their every move: the managers, the physios, the doctors, the nutritionists, the volunteers, the sports scientists, the friends, the families and the partners.

A special thank you to the pioneers of the Winning Scotland Foundation, Graham Watson and Sir Bill Gammell, the visionaries who gave us the go-ahead, both formally and financially, to write *Be a Winner*.

Thanks also to our colleagues at the Foundation, Claire MacDonald, Susan Jackson, Kate Lambie, Ailsa Proverbs, Tommy Boyle and Gregor

Townsend, as well as Alistair Gray, Mike Whittingham and Simon Thomson, who have all imparted their considerable knowledge and expertise in the writing of this book.

Special tribute must be paid to the four women who toiled for hours over our research and manuscripts, putting hundreds of recorded interviews into readable text for us. So thanks to Suzanne Smith, Pamela Gilfillan, Ruth Robertson and Susie Adam.

And we acknowledge our friends in the media – the journalists and press officers who gave us countless names and numbers to help us in our quest to unearth Scotland's sporting heroes. Thanks especially to Elspeth Burnside, Roddy Mackenzie, Adriana Wright, Iain Clark, Rob Eyton-Jones, Colin Hutchison, Matt Lock and Fiona Simpson, who have helped us almost daily in their endeavours.

Of course, we must say thank you to Bill, Iain and the entire team at Mainstream Publishing for their efforts in making us as happy as we are with this book. A great job that we are thoroughly pleased with.

And, finally, thanks to our own friends and family, who after months of listening to our tales must now be convinced that Scotland is on track to becoming the greatest sporting nation on earth. Of course, maybe they're right . . .

Richard Orr and Kenny Kemp

BIBLIOGRAPHY

Armstrong, Lance, *Every Second Counts: From Recovery to Victory* (Yellow Jersey Press, 2003)

Barnes, Simon, *The Meaning of Sport* (Short Books, 2006)

Besford, Pat and Long, Tommy, *Wilkie* (Kemps, 1976)

Bowers, Chris, *Fantastic Federer: The Biography of the World's Greatest Tennis Player* (John Blake Publishing Ltd, 2007)

Busby, Matt, *Soccer at the Top: My Life in Football* (Weidenfeld & Nicolson, 1973)

Campbell, Tom (ed.), *Ten Days that Shook Celtic* (Fort Publishing Ltd, 2005)

Delaney, Terence, *The Footballer's Fireside Book* (Sportsman's Book Club, 1963)

Dick, Frank, *Winning: Motivation for Sport and Business* (Abingdon Management Company Ltd, 1992)

Drysdale, Neil, *Silver Smith: The Biography of Walter Smith* (Birlinn, 2007)

Ferguson, Alex, *Managing My Life: My Autobiography* (Coronet Books, 2000)

Gallacher, Ken, *Slim Jim Baxter: The Definitive Biography* (Virgin Books, 2002)

Gallacher, Ken, *Strachan Style: A Life in Football* (Mainstream Publishing, 1991)

Gordon, Alex, *The Lisbon Lions: The Real Inside Story of Celtic's European Cup Triumph* (Black and White Publishing, 2007)

Hemery, David, *Sporting Excellence: What Makes a Champion?* (Collins Willow, 1991)

Keddie, John, *Running the Race: Eric Liddell, Olympic Champion and Missionary* (Evangelical Press, 2008)

Law, Denis, *The King: My Autobiography* (Bantam Books Ltd, 2004)

MacArthur, Ellen, *Race Against Time* (Penguin Books, 2005)

Magnusson, Sally, *The Flying Scotsman: The Eric Liddell Story* (Quartet, 1981)

Obree, Graeme, *The Flying Scotsman: The Graeme Obree Story* (Birlinn, 2003)

Redgrave, Steve and Townsend, Nick, *Steve Redgrave: A Golden Age – The Autobiography* (BBC Books, 2000)

Reid, Harry, *The Final Whistle? The Strange Death of Scottish Football* (Birlinn, 2005)

Rosaforte, Tim, *Tiger Woods: The Championship Years* (Headline, 2000)

Ross, Andrew, *Alain Baxter: Unfinished Business – The Authorised Biography of Britain's Olympic Skier* (Dewi Lewis Media Ltd, 2005)

Shinar, Yehuda, *Think Like a Winner* (Vermilion, 2007)

Sillitoe, Alan, *The Loneliness of the Long Distance Runner* (Plume, 1959)

Stewart, Jackie, *Winning is not Enough: The Autobiography* (Headline, 2007)

Townsend, Gregor, *Talk of the Toony: The Autobiography of Gregor Townsend* (HarperSport, 2007)

Wallechinsky, David, *The Complete Book of the Olympics* (Aurum, 1996)

Wooden, John and Jamison, Steve, *Wooden on Leadership: How to Create a Winning Organization* (McGraw-Hill, 2005)

Woodward, Clive, *Winning!: The Story of England's Rise to Rugby World Cup Glory* (Hodder & Stoughton, 2004)

INDEX